CONNECTING
TIME

FRANCOIS CARR

CONTENTS

*But you, when you pray, go
into your room, and when
you have shut your door,
pray to your Father who is
in the secret place; and your
Father who sees in secret
will reward you openly.*
Matthew 6:6

INTRODUCTION

*Let the words of my mouth and the meditation of
my heart be acceptable in Your sight, O Lord, my
strength and my redeemer.*
Psalm 19:14

*I have seen the face of Jesus, tell me not of aught
beside; I have heard the voice of Jesus, all my
soul is satisfied.*
S.D. Gordon[1]

I came to know Jesus as my Savior in April 1988 while I
was serving in the National Defence Force of South Africa.
I learned the value of daily devotions as a young believer
and experienced the blessing of meeting with the Lord
early in my Christian walk. I valued the discipline and set
aside time for Bible reading and prayer every day since
I was saved. I am thankful for the foundation it laid in
my understanding and knowledge of God. However, it
was only later that I learned that there is a difference
between reading my Bible, praying, and having an intimate
relationship with God.

As young believers, my wife and I were part of a youth
group that met on Friday evenings to do Bible study,
sing and pray together before going out in pairs into the
streets of Pretoria to distribute gospel tracts and share our
testimony of salvation with others. When we were together

as a group, we always asked one another, 'How are your quiet times?' and 'What is God saying to you?' We kept one another accountable in our discipline of reading the Bible, praying and hearing from God.

Connecting Time is a guideline of gleanings from my own journey to develop a meaningful devotional life, also known as our quiet time. It was during a preaching tour in the Netherlands that I compiled the insights I received from the Lord regarding my own quiet time. It soon became the method I am using during my personal devotional times which I have shared with others and it is still the method I am using today in spending time with Jesus.

Later on I realized that some of these principles were also prevalent in the devotional life of George Müller (one of my mentors) and, most importantly, in the example of the life of Jesus Christ. I have learned a lot about myself and about the Lord Jesus through my times alone with Him. And He continues to teach and guide me every day. No matter who you or what your circumstances are, *connecting* and *spending time with Him* will be a life-changing adventure.

Mentored by Books

I started to read at a very young age and I still love reading books although I believe my love of reading and learning has grown more intense. After accepting Jesus Christ as my Savior, I began to read the biographies and autobiographies of great men of God and spiritual leaders.

The first books I read were *The Spiritual Secret of Hudson Taylor*[2] and the six volumes of *They Knew Their God*[3]. My collection has grown over the years to hundreds of books that contain deep spiritual truths and disciplines. There are several books that I read and reread every year. From each read I gather certain values, insights and principles about vision, leadership, prayer, obedience, forgiveness, faith and perseverance. And because of that I have developed greater intimacy with God and love for His Word, learned how to trust God in and for ministry, and how an effective prayer life can change ministry.

I have seen that all spiritual leaders, especially those who excelled or were endowed with special spiritual power far beyond their peers, had three things in common. First, they *set aside time* every day to spend time and meet with God. Second, they *prayed* and *meditated* often on the Word of God. And third, they truly *entered into a deeper spiritual life* with Jesus.

George Müller

George Müller, known for his work among the orphans of Bristol, is one of the people who mentored me. He is one who continues to 'look over my shoulder,' as his books 'whisper insights, principles and applications from his life and ministry'[4] into my life when I face challenges or encounter situations that bring those principles to mind.

One of the highlights of all my tours through Great Britain was visiting the five buildings that George Müller built by faith. Those buildings have accommodated 10,024 orphans over the years. My visit to the George Müller Orphanage laid the foundation for following in his footsteps, believing and trusting the Lord to provide for us in our lives and ministry. As I stood in Müller's study, I saw his table, his chair and his place of prayer. It was an overwhelming experience to browse through his journal and narratives and to realize that he truly only had God to rely on for his and the orphans' daily needs. It encouraged me to keep on believing, trusting, praying, and expecting God to do for me what He did for Müller.

What made him so successful? It is clear from reading his biography that the secret of his life was his daily appointment with God. He said:

I saw more clearly than ever that the primary business to attend to every day was to have my soul happy in the Lord. The first thing to be concerned about was not how much I might serve the Lord, or how I might glorify the Lord; but how I might get my soul into a happy state, and how my inner man might be nourished. For I might seek to benefit believers, I might seek to bring relief to the distressed, I might in other ways seek to behave as it becomes a child of God in this world and yet not be happy in the Lord, and not be nourished and strengthened in my inner man day by day, as all this might not be attended to in a right spirit.[5]

Pebbles and Jewels

I recently read an Oriental fable that tells the story of three horsemen who traveled through the desert by night. They were unexpectedly confronted by a mysterious person. The stranger told them that they would soon cross a dry riverbed.

'When you arrive there,' he said, 'get off your horses and fill your pockets and saddle bags from the riverbed. At sunrise examine the stones you have picked up. You will be both glad and sorry.'

As the man predicted, the travelers came to a dry stream bed. In a spirit of adventure, they put a few of the many stones they found scattered about into their pockets.

At sunrise the next day they examined the pebbles they had picked up. To their great astonishment they found the stones had been transformed into diamonds, rubies, emeralds and other precious stones. Recalling the statement of the stranger in the desert, they understood what he meant—they were glad for the pebbles they had picked up but sorry that they hadn't taken more.[6]

Likewise, we are often happy and excited to learn new truths from God, and to implement them in our lives. However, we automatically think of all the time we have lost, and not lived to our full potential because we have not taken the time to reflect on the truths of God and apply it to our lives.

This book, *Connecting Time*, is my personal method of enjoying a meaningful devotional time with Him. During the course of my relationship with God, I have tried different methods to make my time with Him as fruitful as possible. Some of these 'perfect' methods have lasted but a few days, weeks or months before they left me frustrated again, and I struggled once again to make time for Him.

Finally, after years of struggle and failure, I discovered a method that works for me. I would like to share it with you. *Connecting Time* consists of an introduction and six easy-to-follow steps that will help you to enjoy a meaningful devotional time with God. Here's the outline of the book:

- Introduction—What is Connecting Time?
- Step 1—Preparing to Meet with God
- Step 2—Opening Prayer
- Step 3—Reading His Word
- Step 4—Writing it Down
- Step 5—Personal Prayer
- Step 6—Personalized Obedience

The insights and principles in this book will guide you in a few simple steps to experience the presence and power of Jesus Christ in an intimate and life-changing way. While *Connecting Time* is not an exhaustive method for a personal devotional time, those who practise these principles will be able to see how 'pebbles' turn into 'jewels' when *connecting* with God. But first, before we take a look at the easy-to-follow steps, we need to understand some basic truths about what *connecting time* is.

May you enjoy and learn from every moment spent in quietness with Jesus, while rediscovering the joy of intimacy with Him and in becoming more like Jesus. I pray that this book will help you see the need for personal quiet time with the Lord and fuel the desire in your heart to set aside true quality time with God. It is also my prayer that it will stir your heart to overcome the various hindrances that keep you from sitting at the feet of Jesus.

You will be happy if you do overcome them.

You will also be full of regret that you hadn't started sooner.

WHAT IS CONNECTING TIME?

Cause me to hear Your lovingkindness in the morning, for in You do I trust. Cause me to know the way in which I should walk, for I lift up my soul to you.

Psalm 143:8

My quiet time is not for a devotional thought, but for a deeper relationship with my Heavenly Father. My quiet time alerts me to what God wants to do in my life the rest of the day.

Henry Blackaby[7]

After finishing a preaching tour in the United Kingdom some time ago, I was waiting at Heathrow Airport in London for my connecting flight to South Africa. From where I was sitting, I could see various runways through the terminal windows. I counted 15 planes on the runway, waiting for their turn to take off. There were also about 10 planes circling in the air, waiting for air traffic control to approve their landing.

I made a few quick calculations and realised that there would roughly be between 12,000 and 15,000 passengers on various airplanes at the airport at any given time. Some were arriving, and others were departing. These numbers do not include those passengers who are not on any aircraft yet, or those who are still going through customs control or are checking in. I also realised that Heathrow was only one of three airports in London. I thought of the other airports in England, Europe, Africa and the rest of the world. There are hundreds of thousands, if not millions, of people flying or traveling every day from one place to another, crossing borders and oceans, going from one country to another. And they can do so within one day. I myself have flown 1,500 to 2,000 km early in the morning several times to speak at a conference and returned home the same day.

Watching the thousands of people at the airport, I thought about the life of C.T. Studd, famous England cricketer, who lived before traveling by airplane was possible. He was born to a wealthy home, educated at Eton and Cambridge, and a successful future was assured for him. However, he stunned the nation by announcing that he was going to China as a missionary with six close friends from Cambridge. Together they became known as the '*Cambridge Seven*.'[8] He gave up his wealth, fame, status and career as a sportsman to work and serve as a missionary. He served alongside Hudson Taylor in China as part of the China Inland Mission. He spent 15 years in China, and 6 years in India, after which he devoted the rest of his life to spreading the gospel message in Africa.

He founded the Worldwide Evangelisation Crusade (now W.E.C. International) and at the age of 70 he still laboured for the Lord at Ibambi in the Congo.[9] His work as a missionary required him to leave his home and family behind in London regularly. He often sailed to Africa, the boat trip and traveling to the mission station taking several weeks, sometimes months. He was therefore away from home for long periods and the extended journeys meant that letters and news often took weeks or even months to be delivered.

It is so very different today.

We can fly or travel to any destination within 24 hours. We can post a message on social media and literally thousands of people can see, read and respond to it within minutes or seconds. We can be in contact with each other, and immediately receive an answer or feedback, through email, text, voice notes, video calls, or even see each other through social media. We are truly living in a global village.

Blessing or Distraction

In 2019 the population of the world was 7,676 billion. About 67% of the total population were mobile users, 57% were internet users, 45% were active on social media and 43% were active mobile social media users. According to the 2019 digital report, the average person spends about 6 hours and 19 minutes per day online.[10] In today's age an average person touches his smartphone 2,617 times per day. A more extreme user taps, touches, scrolls or clicks his phone 5,427 times per day.[11]

> Technology has changed the world as we know it.
> It has also changed the way we think and live.
> We may even be consumed by it.

We live in an instant world; a world with instant coffee, instant food, instant communication, and instant results for everything in our lives. But it has not necessarily made our lives easier ... in some cases it even complicates things.

We complain when the internet is slow, when our laptops take too long to start up, or when people don't respond quickly enough to our emails or requests.

We all like quick-fixes, but it is important for us to understand that quick-fixes do not apply to any matter concerning God. A relationship with God takes time, effort and commitment.

If I travel by car from Johannesburg to Cape Town in South Africa, a distance of about 1,500 km, at a speed of 120 km per hour, I will reach my destination in about 16 hours. If I travel at 130 km per hour, it will probably take me about 14 hours. The faster I move, the faster I will reach my final destination. However, the gravitational forces on the moon produce exactly the opposite. The slower the movements of the man walking on the moon, the faster he will progress. If he moves more quickly, he would progress more slowly, because the movement would work against the gravitational and other forces on the moon.

The technological development and our pursuit of success have the same impact on our spiritual lives. It seems to me that the more we are exposed to information overload, the internet, and the desire to be connected and have the latest gadgets, the less we know or benefit from it.

We have become so consumed by these distractions that we no longer have the time to slow down and become still. We easily fall into the trap of thinking that a Scripture verse on our mobile phones, or a video clip of our favourite pastor or motivational speaker will help us grow and enable us to receive the peace and wisdom we seek. Others might simply rush through their Bible-reading and prayer time without taking the time to sit quietly, meditate upon the truths, commune with the Lord Jesus and enjoy their relationship with Him.

There is no product on the market which provides you with intimacy with God. Even when the holiest person in your life prays for you, it will not give you greater intimacy with God.

Do you think the disciples would have spent three years following, listening and watching Jesus if they could get to know Him just as intimately if Jesus just prayed for them and laid hands on them?

Probably not!

Quiet Time

What is Quiet Time?

With all the demands of life we are inclined to become so intensely occupied that we end up with busy, overcommitted lives in which every minute is scheduled. Because it's hard for us to draw a line in the sand in determining what is truly important, we sometimes fail in our decision-making and eventually have far more on our plates than we can comfortably handle.

S.D. Gordon, in his book *Trysting Time*, explains that a life of victory and power hinges on three things: *an act*, *a purpose* and *a daily habit*. The initial act is that of personal surrender to the Lord Jesus as Master, once and for all. The fixed purpose is to do what will please Him in every single matter, regardless of the consequences. The daily habit is spending some quiet time daily, alone with the Master, over His Word.[12] Gordon continues to say, 'Let the Christian who would have the power of Jesus marking his life see to it that nothing, absolutely nothing, be allowed either to crowd out this habit, or to flurry its spirit of quiet, reverent listening and waiting.'[13]

Sadhu Sundar Singh, the well-known Indian missionary, once said:

> God is quiet. He does not make a noise; therefore, to understand Him we must be quiet ... in the hurry and rush of life God is silent; we have to sit at Christ's feet if we would feel His blessing, and then Heaven will be in our hearts.[14]

The 'daily habit' has been referred to as the devotional life, the morning hour, the morning watch, the still hour, the quiet hour, or a lovers' appointment, to list only a few. Some simply refer to it as *my quiet time*. We must be quiet to hear the voice of God. Quiet time is a time that we deliberately set aside in our day to spend with God. It is when we remove ourselves from the activities, appointments, relationships or things that are competing for our thoughts and concentrate on the person of Jesus Christ.

What is the Purpose of this Meeting?

Many of us live with a sense of guilt because we are neglecting our personal devotional time with God. During the busyness of life and the hectic demands of the day it's easy to let the care of our inner spiritual life fall by the wayside. We try to measure our spirituality by the number of chapters we read in the Bible, or by the number of times we meet with God during the week. If that is the case in your life, you are missing the point of daily devotions.

Meeting with God is a matter of the heart and has nothing to do with what we do, but everything to do with Whom we meet and who we become in His presence. We cannot become the person God wants us to be if we do not spend time with Him.

Bobby Moore, in his book *Your Personal Devotional Life*, explains that quiet time is a time set aside each day for prayer, Scripture reading, meditation, personalizing the Scripture and cultivation of the Spiritual life. He said that the purpose of the devotional life is to meet God ... to experience God ... to worship God ... to commune with God.[15] *Connecting Time* is so much more than just reading the Bible; it is enjoying fellowship and intimacy with God.

As we have seen already, those who have accomplished much for God in their lives, in their own unique and particular calling, were those who spent time with God, and who prepared their hearts for the happenings of the day. I want to be one of those people.

What about you?

When do we Connect with God?

What is the best time to have quiet time? Many people emphasize the importance of starting the day with daily or morning devotions. They believe if the first morning hour is dedicated to the Lord, the day with its responsibilities will be so too. I also believe this.

Depending on your metabolism, work, and current lifestyle, you may be more alert at midday, or even late at night. What matters most of all is to establish a regular time of day when God can speak to you through His Word and you can respond to Him in prayer (see my book *Running on Empty*[16] for more on this topic). Daniel met with God three times per day (Daniel 6:10). David met with God early in the morning (Psalm 5:4). Abraham met with God in the morning (Genesis 19:27). The same 'fellowship-seeking God' is reaching out to us today. When you meet with Him is up to you. Just make sure that you do!

You will not be disappointed.

What will Happen if I do Connect with God?

If you had a friend who loved you, understood you, accepted you, and encouraged you—a friend who relieved your stress and anxiety, took away your guilt, and gave you wisdom and direction for your life—I am sure that you will try to make time to see that person as much as possible.

I know I would.

Jesus is that One Person. He cares so deeply for us and, quite ironically, we never seem to have time for Him. Jesus loves us, He sees the potential in us, and He can give us peace, joy, wisdom, and security in addition to providing us with all the guidance we need in our lives.

The question is, 'Then why do we NOT treasure and prioritize our time with Him?'

The enemy is very much aware of the importance of our quiet times, and he will do anything to try and talk us out of going there. The enemy will use any number of distractions to keep us from our quiet time. It is up to us to find practical ways to connect with God despite the distractions of this world. This is what quiet time is all about. We truly want to spend time with God in order to experience His presence, comfort, and guidance.

I have found that when I enter into His presence, I am able to receive the:

- courage to face my problems and challenges (Isaiah 41:8);
- wisdom to know what to do (James 1:2);
- strength to do what needs to be done (Philippians 4:13);
- faith to believe and trust in Him (Hebrews 11:6);
- patience to wait on and for Him (Isaiah 40:31).

There is also a supernatural change that occurs in our being. Spending time with God actually changes us into the kind of people that we are meant to be and become.

But we all, with unveiled face, beholding as in a mirror the glory of the Lord, are being transformed into the same image from glory to glory, just as by the Spirit of the Lord. (2 Corinthians 3:18)

Here are some more *benefits and blessings* we receive from spending time with God:

- Fellowship and communion (1 Corinthians 1:9)
- Joy (Psalm 33:20–21; 1 John 1: 3–4)
- Peace (Psalm 119:50)
- Deliverance (Psalm 40:1–3)
- Hearing His Voice (John 10)

- Guidance (Psalm 32:8)
- Rest (Matthew 11:28)
- Power (Psalm 27:14; Isaiah 40:31)
- Directing our Hearts
- Prosperity (Psalm 52:8–9)
- Security (Psalm 62:1–2)
- Mercy (Psalm 130:6–8)
- Securing God's presence in our lives (Exodus 33:7–23)
- Seeing life from His perspective (John 4:34)

Some Obstacles and Frustrations

In his book *Time with God*, Peter V. Deison tells the story of Clarence Jones, who ploughed around a large rock in one of his fields for many years. He had broken several ploughshares and a cultivator on it and had grown rather morbid about the rock. After breaking yet another ploughshare, he started thinking of all the trouble the rock had caused him through the years, and he was finally determined to do something about it. When he put a simple crowbar under the rock, he was surprised to discover that it was only six inches thick and that he could easily break up that rock into small pieces. As he was carting it away, he smiled as he remembered all the trouble the rock had caused him and how much easier his life would have been if he had done something about it sooner.

Deison explained that we humans have a tendency to find a way around an obstacle when we are in a hurry. We simply don't want to take the time to deal with it at that moment. Just like the old farmer, we plough around it.[17]

However, if something continues to create problems, we are much better off just taking the time to fix it. It takes time, discipline and perseverance to pursue holiness.

In his book *Soulkeeping*, John Ortberg describes a conversation that he once had with Dallas Willard when he entered a very busy time of ministry. Ortberg called and asked his friend what he needed to do to stay spiritually healthy. Willard replied, 'Hurry is the great enemy of the spiritual life in our day. You must ruthlessly eliminate hurry from your life.'[18]

We all have problems in our quiet times. There are many reasons for that. Bobby Moore, in his book *Your Personal Devotional Life*, highlighted some obstacles and frustrations; and it will be helpful if we take some time to reflect and pray about some of them.[19]

Lack of Discipline

The most popular excuse is, 'I just don't have the time.' All of us have the same number of hours per day. Each of us has 24 hours, 1,440 minutes or 86,400 seconds per day and our management of that time makes all the difference.

Oswald Chambers, author of *My Utmost for His Highest* once said, 'It is impossible for a believer, no matter what his experience, to keep right with God if he will not take the trouble to spend time with God. Spend plenty of time with Him; let other things go, but don't neglect Him.'[20] You must make the choice to discipline yourself and give priority to starting or continuing your daily devotional life.

Lack of Concentration

I find that when I am tired, anxious or burdened I struggle to keep my mind and thoughts from drifting to the cares of the day. To combat that I would stop reading my Bible and read another book until my mind is focused. At other times it helps me to read my Bible aloud, to read a different translation, or to read in English (my native tongue is Afrikaans) as this challenges me to achieve greater focus.

I moreover keep my journal close by to make a note of new learnings to give attention to them later or write down a promise, prayer or Scripture.

Oswald J. Smith observed the *Morning Watch* but he sometimes struggled with drowsiness. He made the following observation:

> For over forty years now I have observed the *Morning Watch*. I begin by reading the Word of God, remembering the words, 'As newborn babes desire the sincere milk of the word, that ye may grow thereby' (1 Peter 2:2). Second, in obedience to Psalm 5:3, 'My voice thou shalt hear in the morning, O Lord: in the morning will I direct my prayer unto thee, and will look up,' I turn to prayer. Third, drowsiness. I used to become sleepy when I wanted to pray. That was because I knelt down and closed my eyes, and put my head on my arms. Years ago I formed a habit of walking when praying. By walking up and down the room I never become drowsy. I am able to keep wide awake. I discovered that when I knelt down and prayed silently, then minutes seemed a long time, but when I prayed out loud and walked, the time went by quickly. By following these methods I have been able to spend hours in prayer, and I have found the *Morning Watch* my strength and my stay. The problems are solved before I meet them. God hears and answers. Instead of letting my circumstances get on top of me and send me to a sanatorium with a nervous breakdown, I am able to keep on top of my circumstances. I know of no greater thrill than the *Morning Watch*.[21]

Disruptions of Regular Routine and Interruptions

This is a major obstacle in our personal devotional life. A change in your regular program, such as vacations or extended travel, can be a great obstacle to deal with. Whatever disrupts your regular life is something you need to deal with. Obviously, anything that causes you to miss a day of your personal devotional time with God is a problem. This time is something that you must protect as if there is nothing more important in life than connecting with God.

Hurry

Hurry is another barrier to quality quiet time. When we rush through our time with God, it can make us feel disconnected from Him. I have learned to continue with my quiet time as long as possible and only stop when I sense that God is finished with me. I find that if I rush my time with Him, I am not prepared for the day, while also being unable to face the trials, tests, temptations or tasks that come my way. I have also found that continuing to rush my devotional time causes me to feel discouraged and often leads to dry spells in my relationship with God.

Not Applying or Personalizing God's Word in your Life

This can be a major obstacle to true quality quiet time. How many times we have read through the Bible is not important. What is important is how many times the Bible has worked its way through us. What does this mean?

The Bible's truths need to be applied and personalized so that they become visible in our lives. If we do not practise what the Bible teaches us, we might as well stop reading the Bible. When we personalize and apply the truths God shows us, we will grow, be refreshed and renewed, and become more closely connected to Him.

Some Biblical Examples of 'Quiet Time'

The Bible is filled with examples of those who met with God on a regular basis. It will be helpful for you to take some time to look at the list of examples and verses from Scripture. You will learn about when, where, how and why these people met with God and what happened as a result. It will be even of more value to us to follow their example.

We read of:

- Abraham. Genesis 19:27; 22:3
- Jacob. Genesis 28:18–22
- Moses. Exodus 34:2
- David. Psalm 5:3; 2 Samuel 7:18–29
- Levites. 1 Chronicles 23:30
- Lover-Husband. Song of Solomon 5:2
- Isaiah. Isaiah 50:4–5
- Jeremiah. Lamentations 3:22–26
- Daniel. Daniel 6:10
- Ezekiel. Ezekiel 12:8
- Habakkuk. Habakkuk 2:1–2
- Jesus. Mark 1:35

In Closing

What made C.T. Studd so unique? He talked with God, and God talked with him. He was faithful in keeping his appointments with God. He had a habit of rising early to meet with God. Despite tremendous challenges and setbacks in his health, he was able to be a blessing to many lost people as he brought very many of them to Christ.

The biography *C.T. Studd Cricketer and pioneer* contains an insight into his usual early morning routine when out in Africa.

Near the foot of the bed was an open log fire on the dried mud floor. At night, a figure could be seen curled up on a native bamboo couch as close to the fire as he could get, for it was his only "blanket."

It was a full-grown man who attended him with the devotion of a woman. He had a stiff leg and so went by the name of "One-leg."

Things would begin to move about 2:30 a.m. or 3:00 a.m. "One-leg" would wake up as regular as clockwork, and the first sound would be the beating of the sticks together to knock off the burnt ends, and then the long gentle phoo-oo-oo, as he blew the sparks into a flame in the expert fashion. Then on with the kettle, and soon a cup of tea would be made. By this time Bwana (Studd) would be awake. The tea is handed to him and "One-leg" goes back to sleep again. A Bible is taken down from the shelf, and Bwana is alone with God. What passed between them in those silent hours was known a few hours later to all who had ears to listen. The meeting in the morning, seldom lasting less than three hours when Bwana took it; his prayers at night lasting from 7:00 p.m. to 10:00 p.m. What he had heard and seen while alone with God in the early morning was poured out from a heart ablaze for the salvation of men, and lips which had been touched with a live coal. He never needed more preparation for his meetings than those early hours. "He talked with God, and God talked with him, and made His Word live to him."[22]

How Do we Spend Time with God?

There is no right or wrong way to spend time with God. However, there are some basic elements that go into quiet time, such as preparation, reading of Scripture, listening to the Holy Spirit, and prayer. Secondly, there are also keys that would give you some direction in meeting with God, such as reason, mental condition, decision, place, time and a quiet heart. I have mentioned this in my book

The Call[23] and discussed it in more detail in *Running on Empty*.[24] Every believer and spiritual leader will develop his or her own habit, system or structure over time.

I have found that I can enjoy a meaningful and effective quiet time by following six easy steps, as mentioned in the Introduction. I hope in following them you will enjoy a meaningful *connecting time* with God. This is my prayer for you.

STEP ONE

PREPARING TO MEET WITH GOD

*And Joshua said to the people: "Sanctify yourselves,
for tomorrow the Lord will do wonders among you."*

Joshua 3:5

*There is no secret to success. It is the result of
preparation, hard work and learning from failure.*

Colin Powell[25]

I've had the privilege of visiting some amazing sites, and
viewing magnificent sights in my life. I've seen the Niagara
Falls in Canada, the architectural wonders of New York
City, participated in dog sledding in the Banff National
Park in the Canadian Rockies, flown over the Alps in New
Zealand, snorkeled with dolphins in the Red Sea, and
hiked on Mount Sinai in Egypt, to name only a few.

But nothing I've ever seen or experienced comes close
to what some of the people saw and experienced in Old
Testament times. Moses and others witnessed the most
breathtaking sight of all time. They had a glimpse of the
glory of God—a visible manifestation of our Lord's invisible
being and character.

Moses encountered God on Mount Sinai and as a result
his face shone (Exodus 34:29; 2 Corinthians 3:18). The
Israelites saw that glory in a cloud (Exodus 16:10). I can
only imagine what this glory might have been like.

The Israelites' Experience
—Exodus 19:1–14; 21; 23

Israel's exodus from Egypt wasn't the end of their experience with God; it was only the beginning. When God spoke to Moses at the burning bush, He gave him an encouraging promise; 'I will certainly be with you. And this shall be a sign to you that I have sent you: When you have brought the people out of Egypt, you shall serve God on this mountain' (Exodus 3:12). That promise had now been fulfilled. They arrived, finding themselves in the shadow of Mount Sinai. They were ready to hear from God, but first Moses had to climb the mountain to hear and receive God's Word.

Charles R. Swindoll, in his book *Moses*, explains that this passage lists four prerequisites God determined for His people before they could meet with Him. He brought them to His chosen meeting place, but before He would give His revelation to them, He required them to do four things.[26]

First, they had to be *willing to obey.*

> And Moses went up to God, and the Lord called to him from the mountain, saying, "Thus you shall say to the house of Jacob, and tell the children of Israel: 'You have seen what I did to the Egyptians, and how I bore you on eagles' wings and brought you to Myself. Now therefore, if you will indeed obey My voice and keep My covenant, then you shall be a special treasure to Me above all people; for all the earth is Mine. And you shall be to Me a kingdom of priests and a holy nation.' These are the words which you shall speak to the children of Israel." So, Moses came and called for the elders of the people and laid before them all these words which the Lord

commanded him. Then all the people answered together and said, "All that the Lord has spoken we will do." So, Moses brought back the words of the people to the Lord. (Exodus 19:3–8)

Second, they had to be *sensitive to listen.*

And the Lord said to Moses, "Behold, I come to you in the thick cloud, that the people may hear when I speak with you and believe you forever." So, Moses told the words of the people to the Lord. (Exodus 19:9)

Third, they had to *sanctify and consecrate their hearts.*

Then the Lord said to Moses, "Go to the people and consecrate them today and tomorrow and let them wash their clothes. And let them be ready for the third day. For on the third day the Lord will come down upon Mount Sinai in the sight of all the people. You shall set bounds for the people all around, saying, 'Take heed to yourselves *that* you do *not* go up to the mountain or touch its base. Whoever touches the mountain shall surely be put to death. Not a hand shall touch him, but he shall surely be stoned or shot *with an arrow*; whether man or beast, he shall not live.' When the trumpet sounds long, they shall come near the mountain." So, Moses went down from the mountain to the people and sanctified the people, and they washed their clothes. (Exodus 19:10–14)

Last, they had to *show deep respect* for God's presence.

And the Lord said to Moses, "Go down and warn the people, lest they break through to gaze at the Lord, and many of them perish." But Moses said to the

Lord, "The people cannot come up to Mount Sinai; for You warned us, saying, 'Set bounds around the mountain and consecrate it.'" (Exodus 19:21, 23)

So, what happened next?

When they were obedient to prepare their hearts for their meeting with God by fulfilling His requirements, He came down and met with them. The Scriptures tell us more about the encounter in Exodus 19:16–19:

Then it came to pass on the third day, in the morning, that there were thunderings and lightnings, and a thick cloud on the mountain; and the sound of the trumpet was very loud, so that all the people who were in the camp trembled. And Moses brought the people out of the camp to meet with God, and they stood at the foot of the mountain. Now Mount Sinai was completely in smoke, because the Lord descended upon it in fire. Its smoke ascended like the smoke of a furnace, and the whole mountain quaked greatly. And when the blast of the trumpet sounded long and became louder and louder, Moses spoke, and God answered him by voice.

Moses' Experience—Exodus 34:1–35

God invited Moses, Aaron, Nadab, Abihu, and 70 of the elders to ascend the mountain (Exodus 24:1–8). Moses and Joshua moved even higher up (vv. 13–14) and only Moses went right up and saw the glory of God (vv. 15–17). It was during this 40-day period that God revealed Himself to Moses and entrusted unto him the blueprint of the Tabernacle's building plans (Exodus 25–31).

His communion with God was interrupted by God's people breaking the Law (Exodus 32). God disciplined them (Exodus 32:35; 3:11) by sending a plague amongst them. God also refused to stay amongst them and took the Tabernacle outside of the camp. Moses pleaded with God to restore His promised blessings to them. In Exodus 34:1–28 we see that God granted forgiveness once again and revealed to them His requirements and expectations.

He also set before Moses a pattern to follow:

- Moses had to cut two tablets of stone (v. 1)
- He had to be ready in the morning (v. 2)
- He had to go into God's presence (v. 2)
- He had to present himself to God on top of the mountain (v. 2)
- He had to come alone (v. 3)
- He obeyed (v. 4)
- God descended to meet with Moses (v. 5)
- He experienced the presence of God (v. 5)
- He prayed (vv. 6–7)
- He worshiped (v. 8)
- He asked and interceded (v. 9)
- God gave directions and instructions (vv. 10–28)
- He wrote down what God told him (v. 27)
- He was transformed in God's presence (vv. 29–34)
- He shared what God told him (vv. 31–32)

Moses was a man who met with God. He heard God speak and he encountered Him intimately. He was obedient to fulfill all the requirements of God. And, as a result, God descended to meet with him and he saw the glory of God (Exodus 34:1–4).

God will meet with us too, if we approach Him in the way He requires.

Approaching God

God called Moses to Mount Sinai (Exodus 24) to give him the blueprint and pattern of the *Tabernacle in the Wilderness* (Exodus 25:40; Hebrews 8:5). The Tabernacle was a way in which God wanted to manifest His presence in the camp (Exodus 25:8; 29:44–46). What a privilege (Romans 9:4–5)!

However, with the Tabernacle in the camp came a responsibility, for it meant that the camp had to be a holy place where a Holy God could dwell.

I once stood at Shiloh and looked toward the general area where the *Tabernacle in the Wilderness* stood for 369 years before it was captured by the Philistines. If we could have flown over the area at the time, the sight we would have seen would've been fascinating. We would have seen the 12 tribes of Israel formed in an outer circle, the families of the Levites would have formed the middle circle, and right in the center or inner area, the *Tabernacle in the Wilderness* would have stood.

During those days a pillar of cloud hovered over the Tabernacle by day and a column of fire by night (Exodus 40:3–38).

It is clear from this design that God was in the midst of His people. In the center He made Himself visible in the cloud and in the fire. They were intended to point the people not only to the One Who 'tabernacled' among them but also to the new path He opened for them, a path into the presence of the unimaginable beauty and glory of God. This is the path to having a relationship and enjoying fellowship with Almighty God. Because the Tabernacle was the dwelling place of God, it was the place the people went to experience the beauty and the wonder of God and His presence. King David longed to be in that presence. He wrote in Psalm 27:4:

One thing I have desired of the Lord, that will I seek:
that I may dwell in the house of the Lord all the days
of my life, to behold the beauty of the Lord, and to
enquire in His temple.

In the New Testament we can easily replace the Tabernacle
with the closet (Matthew 6:6), or our bodies as temples of
the Holy Spirit (1 Corinthians 3:16; 6:19).

Just take a moment and picture the sight in your mind's
eye. Every time when the Israelites walked out of their
house and looked toward the Tabernacle, they would see
the cloud, and be reminded of God's glory and presence.
Likewise, every time when you enter your 'closet' or place
of meeting with God, you will be in the very presence of
God and able to hear His voice (Matthew 6:6; Numbers
7:89). Or, when you take a moment to stop, reflect on
the knowledge that your body has become a temple of
the Holy Spirit, and you will know that you are actually
standing in His presence (Matthew 1:23; 1 Corinthians
3:16).

God is a holy God, and those who approach Him must
do so on His terms. His terms are the only terms that
render us suitable to appear before Him. Any time that we
come to meet with Him or spend some time in the 'closet'
or reading the Bible with the intention to meet with Him,
we need to prepare for such an encounter. My intention is
not to read my Bible, pray or exercise a religious activity
but to experience and encounter Him and to hear from
Him. God told Moses to prepare the people and later on
himself before he came into God's presence.

So should we.

When I make my way toward the 'tabernacle' or 'closet'
to meet with God, I think about my previous time in His
presence.

So, as you come to meet with God, take a moment and
reflect on your previous encounter and ask yourself some
questions:

- What happened during those intimate moments?
- What has God recently said to me (John 14:26)?
- What did He speak to me about?
- Was there a sin that I had to confess?
- Was there something that I had to repent of?
- Was there someone whom I had to forgive?
- Was there an example to follow?
- Was there a command to obey?
- Do I find myself at a place where I will hear something new and have a fresh encounter with Him, or will His voice be quiet as a result of my disobedience?
- Is my heart clean before God?

David wrote:

Who may ascend into the hill of the Lord? Or who may stand in His holy place? He who has clean hands and a pure heart. Who has not lifted up his soul to an idol, nor sworn deceitfully? He shall receive blessing from the Lord. (Psalm 24:3–5a)

Maybe it is time to pray:

Search me, O God, and know my heart; try me, and know my anxieties; and see if there is any wicked way in me and lead me in the way everlasting. (Psalm 139:23–24)

If the Holy Spirit reminds and convicts you of something which is not pleasing to Him, remember:

If we confess our sins, He is faithful and just to forgive us our sins and to cleanse us of all unrighteousness. (1 John 1:9)

Preparing to Meet with God

How do I prepare myself to meet with God? We have already seen that God told Moses to be sensitive, willing to obey, to sanctify himself, and show respect. There are many obstacles and frustrations you will face when starting or even proceeding with your daily devotions. I would like to share with you some thoughts that I have found helpful in my own devotional life.

In my book *The Call*,[27] I highlighted some enemies of intimacy, such as drifting, busyness, distractions and complacency that you should watch out for. Make sure that none of them becomes a quiet-time killer. In my book *Running on Empty*,[28] I explained that you need to find the *right time* to meet with God. God wanted to meet with Moses early in the morning. You also need to find the *right place* to meet. God summoned Moses to come to the top of the mountain, Horeb, also called the mountain of God (Exodus 3:1, 12; 24:1; 34:1). But, most importantly, you need to have *a quiet heart* (1 John 3:18–22).

You also need the *right resources and tools* for an effective and meaningful quiet time. God told Moses to prepare the tablets of stone and bring them with him. You will need an easy-to-read Bible, and a notepad or notebook for writing down your insights and the assignments you receive during your time with God. I also find it helpful to use a daily devotional (see list of recommended resources), a hymnal to sing from and, when I am at home and not traveling, one or two additional Bible translations and commentaries.

Just remember that your devotional time is not study time, but time to worship, read the Scriptures, listen to the Holy Spirt, respond in prayer, and learn to be with Jesus. Study comes later.

However, it is also important to make sure that you are *physically, mentally, emotionally,* and *spiritually* prepared to meet with God.

Physical Preparation

First, ensure that you have had enough *sleep or rest*. Your devotional time starts the previous evening, and if you do not get enough sleep, you will not be able to focus on your time with God. The discovery of electricity has transformed night into day. It causes people to spend more time working at night and therefore our rest times have become shorter. Television, social media, and our busy social programs have further caused cutting of the amount of time set aside for sleep and rest. We therefore get tired sooner and often feel exhausted. When we go to bed late on several consecutive nights, we might oversleep and miss out on our daily time with the Lord. Tiredness affects our concentration, and sometimes we give up or do not 'experience' closeness to or the Presence of the Lord.

Second, ensure that you are *prompt*. I follow a straightforward 'method.' It is the following: I get out of bed. I try to respond promptly when my alarm goes off as I believe that, as many of us know, 'Just five more minutes' often means waking up 30 minutes later. By then the time to connect with God has passed. So, after rising, I wash, shave, brush my teeth and get dressed. I make a cup of coffee and go to my quiet place to have my quiet time with Him. So, I'm entirely awake and can concentrate on what I am about to do. My quiet place is not in or on my bed. I sit in a comfortable chair or even take a walk, if necessary.

Third, deal with *distractions and disruptions*. Distractions are those things that draw our attention away from our quiet time but over which we have control. Disruptions are those things over which we have no control, for example when someone knocks on your door to visit you unexpectedly.

The most common distraction is receiving text messages, video clips or calls on our mobile phones during our quiet time. Many also receive notifications on their phones or emails received on their laptops. In both cases we face the temptation to look at and respond to the 'urgent message' before continuing with our time with the Lord, not realizing that this causes a break in our concentration, and we might easily become disconnected.

I have made a firm commitment not to look at any text messages or emails I receive while I am reading and praying, except for an urgent call from a member of my immediate family. I have also found it helpful to turn off the sound completely. Furthermore, I have set my heart on not starting to work on something urgent or something that needs my attention before I have finished my time with God. This reminds me of Mr. Floyd Banker, who made the commitment 'no prayer, no breakfast.' He was a missionary in Gujerat, India, who experienced a touch from the Lord in revival power during his time in the mission field. He had discovered that the demands on a missionary were myriad and that it was easy to grow careless in keeping the early morning watch. He shared a secret that he had learned:

"Someone may ask, 'What happens when you oversleep, or the alarm clock fails? Are there no exceptions allowed?'" I wish to let you into a secret which has become a very simple rule in our lives and is expressed in four little words: "No prayer, no breakfast." We were brought to this rule early in this new prayer life by a rather strange experience. It so happened one morning that the alarm failed, and we overslept. We went out to our breakfast with the thought that we would find time later in the day for secret prayer, but the cares and burdens of our work pressed in and we forgot. The following morning, we arose in plenty of time for the prayer hour and me and my wife had the same experience. As we went to our separate places of prayer it was if Christ was already there to welcome us but with a sad countenance as He said, "I have waited for you for twenty-four hours."

Like a shock from Heaven this new truth was borne in upon our minds: We had robbed Him of fellowship which He greatly enjoyed. Not only did we benefit from secret prayer, but He also received benefit and great pleasure. So, we have a simple rule: "No prayer, no breakfast."[29]

Mental Preparation

Mental preparation relates to how we get in the right frame of mind for the maximum benefit of our time with the Lord. Moses sat on the mountain for six days before he was invited into God's presence. It gave him some time to quiet his heart and focus on the One Whom he was about to meet. I have found that when my heart is filled with worry about some immediate need or problem, I cannot really focus on or experience the presence of the Lord.

We also need to prepare ourselves against wandering thoughts. If I feel as if my thoughts might wander, I read or pray aloud, go for a walk, or write down my thoughts and prayers in my journal. We should also be aware of boredom or loss of interest, which are also very common occurrences. It could be that we are reading the wrong part of the Bible, or that we need to ask the Lord to help us to focus our hearts anew on what we are reading. It is important to read and study the right book or passage of Scripture, otherwise it might become a wasted read or you may not remember what you had been reading. It is sometimes helpful to change the translation of the Bible you are reading for a couple of days.

Emotional Preparation

I have learned over the years that guilt, anger or fear will dominate your thoughts, focus and concentration until it is dealt with. When you find that your heart is not at ease, that you struggle to concentrate, and you cannot trace it back to a physical or mental cause, this is the best place to check. We must remember when we committed a sin against God, the Holy Spirit will convict us of sin, righteousness and judgment (John 16). However, we might also struggle with false guilt because of legalism, or expectations that have not been met.

Spiritual Preparation

It may be that we have committed a sin against God and we have to deal with it before we will receive something new and fresh from God (see Psalms 24; 66:18). Apart from sinning against God of our own will, we also have a spiritual enemy who wants to destroy us. Jesus spoke of him as a real foe. Our enemy knows that a growing relationship with the Lord is the greatest threat to his plot to destroy us. He will try to deceive you and occupy you with things that will continue to keep you busy and unprepared to meet with God.

In Closing

The devotional life connects the inner life of a person to the very presence of God Himself. The devotional life enables a person to receive all he or she needs for a life of fulfilment and purpose. But how does that connection happen? First, you need to *prepare yourself* before or when you approach your quiet time to get the most out of it.

Second, you must *spend unhurried quiet time* with the Lord. God is never in a hurry. Third, you must remember that you have *come to meet* with the Master, the Creator of the Universe, the Author of the Bible, and the One Who holds your life in the hollow of His Hand. You are meeting with Him to get to know Him better, listen to His voice, realize His presence, look into His face, and just be with Him. You must prepare yourself before you approach God otherwise you will just go through the motions of a religious exercise and miss out on hearing from Him.

In the quiet of the dawning,
alone with Him I love.
The stillness of His presence
brings perfume from above.
It sweetens all the hours
of my coming busy day.
Its fragrance calms my restlessness
and drives my fear away.
I find wondrous strength for duty
as I look into His face,
And I know that there is power drawn
from this secret place.

J. Charles Stern[30]

STEP TWO
OPENING PRAYER

Come up to Me on the mountain and be there.
Exodus 24:12

*Be still and know that God is within thee and round.
In the hush of the soul the unseen becomes visible
and the eternal real. The eye dazzled by the sun
cannot detect the beauties of its perihelion till it has
had its time to rid itself of the glare. Let no day pass
without its season of silent waiting.*
F.B. Meyer[31]

God invited Moses, Nadab, Abihu, and 70 of the elders to ascend the mountain and be with Him (Exodus 24:1–8). They responded to the invitation, left the camp and ascended the mountain. We read in Exodus 24:9–11:

Then Moses went up, also Aaron, Nadab, and Abihu, and seventy of the elders of Israel, and they saw the God of Israel. And *there was* under His feet as it were a paved work of sapphire stone, and it was like the very heavens in its clarity. But on the nobles of the children of Israel He did not lay His hand. So, they saw God, and they ate and drank.

Because of their obedience they saw God and had fellowship with Him. Then God extended an invitation to

Moses and summoned him to meet with Him further up
the mountain. God wanted to give Moses the Law so that
he could teach it to his people. Moses obeyed and took
his assistant Joshua with him, while the elders waited for
them, as written in Exodus 24:12–14.

> Then the Lord said to Moses, "Come up to Me
> on the mountain and be there; and I will give you
> tablets of stone, and the Law and commandments
> which I have written, that you may teach them." So,
> Moses arose with his assistant Joshua, and Moses
> went up to the mountain of God. And he said to the
> elders, "Wait here for us until we come back to you.
> Indeed, Aaron and Hur are with you. If any man has
> a difficulty, let him go to them."

Moses left Joshua, went up into the midst of the cloud into
the mountain, and stayed on the mountain for 40 days and
40 nights, which we read in Exodus 24:15–18.

> Then Moses went up into the mountain, and a cloud
> covered the mountain. Now the glory of the Lord
> rested on Mount Sinai, and the cloud covered it six
> days. And on the seventh day He called to Moses out
> of the midst of the cloud. The sight of the glory of
> the Lord *was* like a consuming fire on the top of the
> mountain in the eyes of the children of Israel. So,
> Moses went into the midst of the cloud and went up
> into the mountain. And Moses was on the mountain
> forty days and forty nights.

God waited for six days before He spoke to Moses. He
only called him on the seventh day to enter into His
presence. Moses did not do anything, he was still, quiet
and in solitude. He was waiting on God to speak to him
and reveal what was on His heart. Why did God make him

wait? I believe that God wanted him (and us) to learn two very important principles:

- The principle of *being there* or *present*.
- The principle of *directing our hearts*.

Be There

A few years ago, I preached in Namibia and was able to visit the famous Fish River Canyon. It is the largest canyon in Africa and the second largest in the world after the Grand Canyon in the USA. It is about 160 km long, 27 km wide at some places and 550 m deep. When I arrived, there was a group of young people who were having a party, drinking, listening to music, laughing loudly. It had taken me almost two hours to get there that morning and wanted to enjoy the majesty of it all. I was disappointed that this group was there and that their focus was not the beauty of the canyon but clearly elsewhere.

I have to confess I was not very happy about them and asked the Lord either to keep them quiet or to remove them. I am not sure if it was my prayer or not, but they left soon after that. After they had departed, I was able to sit in complete silence and look down into the ravine. At one point the silence was so intense it gave me an earache. As I sat there and enjoyed the quietness, I was reminded of Moses who waited on God for six days.

God told Moses in Exodus 24:12, 'Come up to Me on the mountain and *be there*.' What does it mean, and how does that apply to us today? Lois Tverberg, in her book *Reading the Bible with Rabbi Jesus*, shares the explanation of a nineteenth-century rabbi, who points out that there is, in fact, such as a thing as going to a place and not actually being there in this comment of his:

> If a person exerts himself and ascends to the summit, it is possible to reach it, while not being there. He

stands on the summit of the mountain, but his head is somewhere else.[32]

Lois Tverberg added, 'It's entirely possible for a person to expend a great deal of energy getting to a destination yet arrive there with their head and thoughts remaining at the point of departure. The rabbi imagined that God was telling Moses not only to ascend the mountain but to be there fully, with complete attention and concentration, leaving behind all of his extraneous thoughts. On the momentous occasion of the giving of the covenant, God wanted Moses to be fully present, in body, mind, and spirit.'[33]

Later on God told Moses, '*And there* I will meet with you, and I will speak with you' (Exodus 25:22), and when God summoned him, 'So, be ready in the morning, and come up in the morning to Mount Sinai, and *present yourself* to Me' (Exodus 34:2), he knew exactly what that meant. God wanted to meet with him. God wanted to speak to him, but he needed to *be there* and *be present*.

The sons of Korah knew that God was their refuge, strength, a present help and a safe place to hide, Who was ready to help when they needed Him (Psalm 46:1). And because of that they had learned to be still and rest in the knowledge that God is God. We read in Psalm 46:10:

Be still and know that I am God. I will be exalted among the nations. I will be exalted in the earth.

Eugene Peterson captured the essence of this verse in *The Message* as follows:

Step out of the traffic! Take a long, loving look at me, your High God, above politics, above everything.

What about you?

It's time to step out of the traffic.
It's time to take a long, loving look at God.
It's time to remove all distractions ... everything.
It's time to *be there*.

Sadly, many people are not 'there' or present when they are together with other people. We see too many couples enjoying a meal or a coffee together without being aware of one another's presence because of the distractions occupying them. They are constantly glancing at or watching something on their mobile phones. The same is also true for families at home and around the kitchen table. Family members are distracted and miss out on the blessing of just being together. If that is the case, it's time to become intentional with our devotion or focusing the direction of our hearts. The apostle Paul encourages us, 'And whatever you do, do it heartily, as to the Lord and not to men' (Colossians 3:23).

Wherever you are, *be all there* for God.
Whatever you do, *be all there* for God.

Directing my Heart

Lois Tverberg, in her book *Listening to the Language of the Bible*,[34] explained that the Jewish rabbis developed a concept, known as *kavanah*, that can help us to experience God more intimately when we are praying. The word means 'direction,' 'intention,' or 'devotion,' and the idea behind praying with *kavanah* is that you set the direction of your heart toward God and toward praying with all of your heart. A person who has *kavanah* focuses their entire being on prayer and is not distracted by the chaos around them.

In every Jewish synagogue there is an ark (an ornate wall cabinet) that holds the Torah scrolls, and above it there is often a plaque that displays the words '*Know Before*

Whom You Stand.' Kavanah also means to have a sense of being in the presence of God, to know that you are addressing the sovereign Lord of the universe.

Prayer is so simple, and God so familiar to us that it is easy to pray halfheartedly, letting our minds wander off, drifting back to our own thoughts. We may even pray before going to bed and fall asleep halfway through our prayer. It is important to remember that God deserves our best efforts, not meagre efforts. We should live each hour of every day with the awareness of God's presence all around us. Lois Tverberg concludes that if we do this, our lives will be a reflection of Christ, whose desire was to please His Father in every way.[35]

Nicolas Herman was a monk who worked in the kitchen of a monastery in Paris. He became known as Brother Lawrence, the inspirer of a little book entitled *The Practice of the Presence of God*. He once said, 'Consider God as the goal of all your thoughts and desires.'[36] The principle of *kavanah* helps us to live life forward, with our eyes and hearts fixed on Him as our only goal.

Charles Swindoll, in his book *Intimacy with the Almighty*, explained 'Noise and words and frenzied, hectic schedules, closing our ears to His still, small voice and making us numb to His touch.'[37] He continues, 'Noise and crowds have a way of siphoning our energy and distracting our attention, making prayer an added chore rather than a comforting relief.'[38] God does not speak to those who have hurried minds and hearts. God wanted Moses to be alone and silent in order for him to refocus his heart and attention on the One Who had invited him into His presence.

Now I want to tell you a beautifully illustrated story I once read of a man whose artist friend asked him to come to his home and see a painting he had just finished. When he got to his friend's house an attendant showed him into a dark room and left him there. He quietly waited for his friend to come down to meet him. After perhaps 15 minutes his friend came into the room with a cordial greeting and took him up to the studio to see the painting. The painting was magnificent. Before he left, the artist laughingly asked, "I suppose you thought it queer to be left in the dark room for so long." "Yes," his guest said, "I did." "Well," his friend replied, "I knew that if you came into my studio with the glare of the street in your eyes that you would not be able to appreciate the fine colouring of the painting. So, I left you in the dark till the glare had worn out of your eyes."[39]

It is exactly the same with us. We need to refocus our hearts and attention on the One Who invites us into His presence.

David understood the importance of waiting upon the Lord (Psalm 5:3), so did the sons of Korah as well as Moses.

As we begin our quiet time, we must do our very best to direct our hearts to *Know Before Whom We Stand*, and to *be there*.

In Closing

I usually begin my quiet time with a short prayer to become still and set my heart on God. I thank God for a good night's rest, the blessing of a new day and the opportunity to meet and spend some time with Him. The intention of this prayer is to quiet down my heart and tune in to God's voice. We have already seen from the example of Moses that we need to *be there* and *direct our hearts to know before Whom we stand*. We cannot hear from God or receive the riches He has for us if we are not in a position to receive it. I simply ask God to speak to me and to reveal His will for me through His Word. God knows my heart, my needs and my desires.

After praying what I call my *opening prayer*, I use the first few moments just to sit in silence, quietly, allowing the Holy Spirit to speak to me. There are days when I feel that my heart is not focused on the Lord, and it feels as if I am not making contact with Him. I have found that it is usually for one of the following reasons:

First, it may be that I am *tired or not fully rested*.

Second, it may be that there are *underlying concerns, fears or anxieties* filling my heart and mind. We can step into the calming presence of the Lord and find the strength to continue. As we pray about our heartaches and troubles, He meets us where we are and gives us peace. He is an ever-present help, Who cares for us in every situation (Psalm 46:1).

Third, God may remind me of *things that are not pleasing to Him*, and I would take the time to acknowledge them, agree with God that it is sin, confess it as a sin, and ask Him to forgive me and help me not to do it again (see my book on *Spiritual Breathing*).[40]

On the other hand, there are also days and times that He would remind me of what He is doing in my life and I would take some time to reflect on that and thank Him for it.

King David wrote in Psalm 5:3, 'My voice You shall hear in the morning, O Lord. In the morning I will direct it to You, and I will look up.' He prayed and waited with expectation for the Lord to answer. What did he do while he was waiting? The answer is found in in 2 Samuel 7:18–29.

- He sat before the Lord to gain perspective (v. 18).
- He remembered and considered the blessings of the Lord in the past (vv. 18–21).
- He reflected on the nature of God (vv. 22–24).
- He remembered all the promises God had made (vv. 25–28).
- And, finally, he made known his desire and requests unto the Lord (v. 29).

Sometimes I feel like singing a song and worshiping Him. There are moments that I feel the need to read my journal, or my daily devotional book (see recommended reading list).

At times, I watch a short video clip or message. The intention is to slow down the pace, quiet my heart, conquer my fears, take my thoughts captive and focus on Him.

It prepares my heart to read the Bible.

Once my heart is quiet and set on the Lord, I immediately start reading my Bible, while listening to what His Word is telling me for the day.

A Prayer

Lord Jesus, thank you for a good night's rest and that I can feel refreshed this morning. Thank you for protecting and keeping us safe throughout the night, and for adding a new day to our lives. Thank you for the privilege and opportunity to spend some time with You. Lord, you know my heart and my needs this morning. You also know what is written on my prayer list, in my journal and on my bucket list. You also know what is on Your heart and agenda for me for today, and how my life is connected to Your purposes. Lord Jesus, as I come before You today, I pray that You will speak to me, and help me to hear Your voice, and see and understand Your Word, ways and purposes. Help me to live and be the person that I was meant to be. May You be glorified in our time today. In Jesus' name I pray. Amen.

STEP THREE
READ FROM HIS WORD

*Blessed is the man who walks not in the counsel of
the ungodly, nor stands in the path of sinners, nor
sits in the seat of the scornful; but his delight is in
the Law of the Lord. And in His Law, he meditates
day and night. He shall be like a tree planted by
the rivers of water, that brings forth its fruit in
its season, whose leaf also shall not wither; and
whatever he does shall prosper.*
Psalm 1:1–3

*The entrance of Your words gives light; It gives
understanding to the simple.*
Psalm 119:130

Years ago I traveled through Great Britain on a revival
and heritage tour, and visited all the places that are
linked to past revivals and great spiritual leaders. One of
the places we visited was the Bible College of Wales in
Swansea, where Rees Howells and later his son, Samuel
Rees Howells, were the principals. They are well known for
their lives of intercessory prayer. We took a tour through
the main building and were able to spend some time in the
famous blue room, where they usually met to pray. One of
the staff members, an elderly lady, showed me five folders,
each one of them a handwritten copy of the Bible, written

by herself, from the book of Genesis all the way through to the last chapter of the book of Revelation. I realized how many hours she must have spent in the Word of God as she wrote and memorised the passages. When I held those folders and browsed through them it felt as if I was holding 'a sacred book' in my hands. I was convicted of my own lack of commitment and dedication to the Bible.

It reminded me of an important qualification of a king (a spiritual leader). A king had to have personal knowledge of the Law of God. He had to write out his own copy of the Law (Deuteronomy 17:18–20), read it regularly and take it to heart. The study of the Law would not only help him to rule the people justly but would also reveal to him the character of God and encourage him to fear Him and love Him more. It would keep him humble and honest in his doings as he used the authority the Lord had given him. We read in Deuteronomy 17:18–20:

> Also, it shall be, when he sits on the throne of his kingdom, that he shall write for himself a copy of this Law in a book, from *the one* before the priests, the Levites. And it shall be with him, and he shall read it all the days of his life, that he may learn to fear the Lord his God and be careful to observe all the words of this Law and these statutes, that his heart may not be lifted above his brethren, that he may not turn aside from the commandment *to* the right hand or *to* the left, and that he may prolong his days in *his* kingdom, he and his children in the midst of Israel.

We must be readers of God's Word. We must be students of God's Word. We must spend time in the Word of God until we are saturated in its truths. It is when we permeate ourselves with the Word of God that we truly connect with and encounter God.

Encountering God

It was when Moses entered the *midst of the cloud on the mountain* that he encountered God.

> Then the Lord said to Moses, 'Come up to Me on the mountain and be there; and I will give you tablets of stone, and the Law and commandments which I have written, that you may teach them.' (Exodus 24:12)

It was when Moses entered the *Tabernacle of the Wilderness* that he encountered God.

> So it was, whenever Moses went out to the tabernacle, *that* all the people rose, and each man stood at his tent door and watched Moses until he had gone into the tabernacle. And it came to pass, when Moses entered the tabernacle, that the pillar of cloud descended and stood at the door of the tabernacle, and *the Lord* talked with Moses. (Exodus 33:8–9)

> Now when Moses went into the tabernacle of meeting to speak with Him, he heard the voice of One speaking to him from above the mercy seat that *was* on the ark of the Testimony, from between the two cherubim; thus, He spoke to him. (Numbers 7:89)

It was when Moses ascended *Mount Sinai* once again that God came down to meet with him and speak to him, revealing what Moses needed to do next.

> So, he cut two tablets of stone like the first *ones*. Then Moses rose early in the morning and went up Mount Sinai, as the Lord had commanded him; and he took in his hand the two tablets of stone. Now

the Lord descended in the cloud and stood with him there and proclaimed the name of the Lord. (Exodus 34:4–5)

It was on the mountain and in *God's presence* that Moses was changed and transformed.

Now it was so, when Moses came down from Mount Sinai (and the two tablets of the Testimony *were* in Moses' hands when he came down from the mountain), that he, Moses himself, did not know that his face shone while he talked with Him. So, when Aaron and all the children of Israel saw Moses, behold, his face was shining, and they were afraid to come near him. Then Moses called to them, and Aaron and all the rulers of the congregation returned to him; and Moses talked with them. Afterward all the children of Israel came near, and he gave them as commandments all that the Lord had spoken with him on Mount Sinai. And when Moses had finished speaking with them, he put a veil over his face. But whenever Moses went in before the Lord to speak with Him, he would take the veil off until he came out; and he would come out and speak to the children of Israel whatever he had been commanded. And whenever the children of Israel saw the face of Moses, that Moses' face shone, then Moses would put the veil on his face again, until he went in to speak with Him. (Exodus 34:29–35)

It is clear from these Scriptures that God calls us; He invites us to come to Him. When we respond to His call, we receive from Him when He communicates truths from His Word. When we reflect, apply and personalize the truths of His Word we are changed and our lives transformed.

> But we all, with unveiled face, beholding as in a mirror the glory of the Lord, are being transformed into the same image from glory to glory, just as by the Spirit of the Lord. (2 Corinthians 3:18)

Moses was at the right place to receive that which the Lord wanted to give him. He also had the right frame of mind and a listening heart. Moses was *there*, and his *kavanah* was to meet with God. When Moses entered to receive God's Word, he found that God was waiting for him. The ultimate goal of our devotional time is to enjoy true fellowship and communion with God and hear what God will say. It takes place when God comes down to meet with us, speak to us through His written Word. It helps us to secure His presence in our lives, to be changed and transformed into the image of Jesus, to be able to live and act like Him and accomplish His purposes.

Second, it is to realize that our time in God's presence, or in God's Word, should be an 'encounter with God.' When we spend time with God, or time in the Word, we are actually meeting and spending time with the Author of the Bible. Andrew Murray cautioned that all believers run a certain risk 'of substituting prayer and Bible study for living fellowship with God, the living interchange of giving Him your love, your heart, and your life, and receiving from Him His love, His life, and His Spirit.' He warned that we may get so occupied with praying for our own needs, or so absorbed in our Bible study that we never enter into God's presence at all. Indeed, our devotional times in God's Word can end up becoming a substitute for God Himself. This is a great hindrance because it keeps the soul occupied instead of leading it to God Himself. And we go out into the day's work without the power of an abiding intimate fellowship.[41]

When I was a young Christian, I once read of a man of God who read through the Bible eight times in one year.

I thought it was possible and decided to do the same. I had to read about 30 to 32 chapters per day in order to accomplish my goal. I started to read and kept on reading the chapters, despite my full daily program and busy life. I kept going at it for about six months and was pleased that I could keep it up. By that time I had already read through the Bible four times. However, I felt out of contact with God, my spiritual life was dry, and my Bible reading and time with God had become mechanical. When I missed a day and fell behind, I struggled with feelings of guilt, and confessed my 'sin' of not reading my 32 chapters that day.

I lost my peace, and eventually realized that God wasn't asking of me to read through those chapters. He was asking me to be with Him and enjoy intimacy with Him.

The question to ourselves that we must all answer is not whether we have prayed or read our Bibles but whether God 'comes down' to speak to us when we read our Bibles. If not, we have merely exercised a religious activity by ticking off 'devotions' from our list without meeting with God. My experience changed my perspective on spending time with God in His Word. The realization caused me to set my heart on a course to know and encounter God more intimately, instead of just praying and reading the Bible as a religious activity.

The Holy Spirit

God speaks to us through the Holy Spirit (see *The Call*[42] for greater detail on how God speaks to us today). He is to be our Guide, Helper, Teacher, Reminder, Convictor, Truth, Who helps us to glorify Christ. There are seven words that describe the work of the Holy Spirit in the life of a believer. He is the One Who Seals, Reveals, Empowers, Releases, Transforms, Unites and Anoints. He is ultimately sent to be engaged in our everyday lives. God intended our relationship with Him to be intimate as we grow in our walk with Him. He is interested in transforming us from the inside out. His nearness sets that in motion.

He is at work in dozens of different ways, some of them supernatural. He is interested in showing us the Father's will. He stands ready to provide us with the dynamics necessary for experiencing satisfaction, joy, peace, and contentment despite of our circumstances. With the indwelling Spirit, we have all the resources necessary to complete our assignments and accomplish His purposes. He:

- will remind us of all that Jesus said in His Word (John 14:26);
- will teach us all things that Jesus taught (John 14:26);
- will convict us of sin and any wrongdoing in our lives (John 16:7–10);
- will convince us that Jesus is Lord (John 16:7–10);
- will reveal to us and guide us to spiritual truth (John 16:3);
- will show us things to come (John 16:13);
- will reveal God's perspective of our situation;
- will work in our lives to exalt and glorify Jesus to the world around us;
- will help you to do things which are impossible to do on our own.

Listening to the Holy Spirit

We need the Holy Spirit to understand and apply the truths received from God's Word. He enters our life with the initial work of salvation and continues to change us and to transform us into the image of Jesus Christ.

When Jesus began His public ministry, the Spirit descended upon Him like a dove (Luke 3:22). Jesus depended on the Spirit of God for His ministry. Jesus told His disciples what the role of the Holy Spirit would be. He said that He would pray and ask the Father to send another Helper to come and remain with them forever.

> And I will pray the Father, and He will give you another Helper, that He may abide with you forever— the Spirit of truth, whom the world cannot receive, because it neither sees Him nor knows Him; but you know Him, for He dwells with you and will be in you. I will not leave you orphans; I will come to you. (John 14:16–18)

Jesus said, 'However, when He, the Spirit of truth, has come, He will guide you into all truth; for He will not speak on His own *authority*, but whatever He hears He will speak; and He will tell you things to come' (John 16:13).

The Holy Spirit was sent to guide us in all truth.

He is the One Who speaks to us through Scripture. We must learn how to be sensitive to His voice. The Holy Spirit can help you to understand a truth in God's Word; He can help you to understand God's promptings; and He can lead you to confess to or worship God. I have found it helpful to listen by doing two simple exercises.

Exercise 1—Confession

I want you to close your eyes. Look back over the past 24, 36 and 48 hours of your life. Replay the events of the past few days and allow the Holy Spirit to speak to you. Let Him remind you of all those times that you said or did things that were not pleasing to Him. As the memories surface, focus on them and confess them one by one before God as the Holy Spirit brings them to mind. Ask Him to forgive you, restore you and give you His peace. Do not pray a general prayer but deal with each thought individually. There is no time limit, but you might start by setting your alarm for a few minutes and continuing until it goes off.

Exercise 2—Worship and Give Thanks

I want you to close your eyes. Look back over the past 24, 36, and 48 hours of your life. Replay the events of the past few days and allow the Holy Spirit to speak to you. Let Him remind you of all those blessings, provisions, and so forth that God in His mercy and grace bestowed upon you. As the memories surface, focus on the good things that have happened to you. Relive them in your imagination and be thankful for them. Recognize them for what they are: signs of God's encompassing and attentive love for you as His child. Thank Him for it. Do not pray a general prayer but deal with each thought individually. There is no time limit, but you might start by setting your alarm for a few minutes and continuing until it goes off.

Be careful not to take the presence of the Holy Spirit in your life for granted. Ask the Lord to keep doing all those things in your life that you cannot do for yourself. Ask Him for sensitivity for Him. Then pay attention to what He is doing in your life or what He is saying as He takes the Scriptures and guides you in all truth.

How Do I Read and Listen?

It is important to remember that any time invested in reading the Bible will yield eternal rewards, 'for the word of God is living and powerful' (Hebrews 4:12).

How do I read my Bible and listen to the Holy Spirit? Let me give you some suggestions from my own devotional time.

Daily Devotional

First, I read the portion for the day in my daily devotional book. The intention is not to hear from God, although the Holy Spirit sometimes uses the text and the supporting Scriptures to speak, guide and direct my thoughts. The intention is to slow my pace, quiet my heart and cultivate a listening spirit so that I can hear what God says when I read His Word. There are inspiring devotionals to choose from. Over the years I have used *My Utmost for His Highest*,[43] *Streams in the Desert*,[44] *Experiencing God Day by Day*,[45] *Our Daily Bread*[46] and others.

The Bible

Second, I read my Bible. I do not consider the Bible as just another historical book. It is the Word of God that is living and powerful. I do not read the portion of Scripture for the day as part of my preparation for a sermon that I am preparing to preach. I read the Bible for my own spiritual growth and guidance for circumstances as it relates to my life or current circumstances. I also do not use this time as Bible study time—that comes later. I approach the Bible from the perspective of and intention to meet the Author. I have found that if I start with the expectation to hear God speak, I am more attuned to listening to Him and hearing from Him.

Yes, I follow *a system*. You and the Lord must work out the system that is best for you, because He knows your life, routine and responsibilities. But let me give you some suggestions. I like to read through the whole Bible at least once a year. You can read two chapters from the Old Testament and one chapter from the New Testament. Or you can start at Genesis 1, Psalm 1, and Matthew 1, and read one chapter per day and just keep on reading. However, whatever method you use, it is important to reflect and meditate on the verses. You might not read through all of your chapters every day as the Holy Spirit may stop and draw your attention to some point in particular. Some days you might read more chapters, when nothing in particular requires your specific attention. I currently tend to read the Old Testament once, and the New Testament and Psalms twice a year. There are several good Bible reading calendars available, so look for one at your local bookstore or ask your pastor to recommend one. The Bible Reading Plan of Robert Murray M'Cheyne[47] is an excellent calendar to follow.

You might wonder which *Bible translation* to use. The Bible is available in a wide range of translations. I would suggest an easy-to-read Bible translation with plenty of room to make notes. I am currently using the *King James Version* as well as the *Amplified Bible* and *The Message* in my devotions, but you might prefer some other versions that are available. Visit your local bookstore or ask your pastor to recommend a translation that will work well for you. There are a wonderful variety of translations to choose from.

Where to begin? If you are a new believer, I would suggest that you read the Gospel of John first. Once you have done that, begin reading from Matthew and continue through the New Testament before you start reading through the Old Testament. It is important to continue reading where you stopped the last time as it helps you to gain a holistic idea of the book you are reading as well as where it fits in the Bible as a whole.

What to do? You must read the Bible for quality and not quantity. It's good to have a goal to read through the Bible in a year, but do not make the same mistake as I did, and try to read 32 chapters every day. The purpose of your time in the Bible is to meet the Author, to hear from Him with an open mind, and to listen. He knows all about you, but you and I need to know a lot more about Him. Do not read your Bible as if this is something that you have to do. If that is the case it becomes an obligation, and a burden. Rather see it as an opportunity that brings you a blessing. Warren Wiersbe[48], in his book *God Isn't In A Hurry* explains that spending time daily with Jesus in the Word and prayer should be an experience to enjoy, and not an event to endure. If we do our quiet time can become quite a time.

Holy Spirit

Third, I pay close attention to the portion of Scripture I read during my quiet time and listen to hear if the Holy Spirit is showing me an insight, promise, correction, or encouragement, or revealing, guiding or convicting me in any way. My intention is to hear from God. I will read until I sense God is speaking to me or revealing His heart and agenda. Allow me to give you some practical examples.

- *Conviction*. Sometimes when I read my Bible, I experience a great sense of sorrow and the conviction of sin in my heart. If I ask the Holy Spirit to shed light on these emotions, He reveals something in my life that is not pleasing to Him. I would stop reading and pray a prayer of confession (see my book *Spiritual Breathing*).[49]

- *Petition.* Sometimes when I am reading my Bible, the face or picture of someone or a situation will come to mind. The Holy Spirit would impress upon my heart to pray for that person. I would stop reading and pray a prayer of petition for that person.

- *Worship and Thanks.* Sometimes when I am reading my Bible, my heart is filled with joy and gladness. The Holy Spirit reminds me of all goodness, kindness, blessings, provisions, or His answers to my prayers. I would stop reading and pray a prayer of thanksgiving.

- *New Insights.* Sometimes when I am reading my Bible, God will draw my attention to a verse or passage in the Scriptures. It is as if the verse is written in bold letters as it stands out. I would look at the various references about the same verse and consult other translations. I would ask several questions (see steps 4 to 6 for more detail) and reflect upon that. I would also study the passage by looking at the context of the Bible book in greater detail. I would stop reading and pray about what I have read and ask the Holy Spirit to apply and personalize the truth of this Scripture in my life.

You might ask, 'What is the reason for me to stop reading the Bible and praying so many times? Should I not finish my reading and my devotional time before I pray at the end?' The answer is no. The purpose of your devotional time is to commune with God. Communication is a two-way conversation which includes prayer (speaking to Him) and listening (hearing from Him). If God speaks to you, it is crucial to respond to Him. When you stop reading to pray in response to what He has revealed to your heart, you are focusing on what the Lord is showing you. It is a form of obedience. We need to respond immediately otherwise the moment might be lost and we might delay responding to Him, and that leads to being disobedient. I want to please Him, and keep His commandments, as it positions me for my next encounter with Him.

And whatever we ask we receive from Him, because we keep His commandments and do those things that are pleasing in His sight. (1 John 3:22)

You might ask, 'how long or how much time do I spend in His presence?' When you are reading the Bible and praying, you should stay there until you experience the release from God that your time with Him is over. You might have to stay until you receive a fresh word from Him, the peace that you have been forgiven for a sin you have committed or instructions and guidelines for your day and life. You should also be able to read enough to get to know Jesus more intimately and to be changed and transformed into His image. The amount of time that I spend in the Word depends on what God is impressing on my heart. There are times that I am just reading the portion of Scripture for the day, and then there are other times that I only stop when He releases me.

In Closing

As God guides you to understanding His truth, write it down, meditate on it, and adjust your life to what you have heard. When you conclude your quiet time, look to see how His Word applies to your life as you go through the day. He does not reveal truth randomly; everything is connected to His ways and purposes. He sees the bigger picture.

What God is saying to you today is because of what He knows lies ahead. He is preparing you to be victorious over anything that you might face. If things are not clear and you get confused, run into God's presence, to His Word and ask Him to bring clarity to your situation.

Remain in His presence until you receive the light you need. Remember, one of the goals of your devotional time is to secure the presence of God throughout the day.

STEP FOUR

WRITE IT DOWN

What you see, write in a book ...
Revelation 1:11

Write the things which you have seen, and the things which are, and the things which will take place after this.
Revelation 1:19

Several years ago, I traveled through Turkey and Greece in the footsteps of St. Paul and St. John. I was especially excited to visit the island of Patmos, where John was exiled for 18 months, and the cave where St. John wrote the book of Revelation. He wrote the book of Revelation about A.D. 95, during the reign of the Roman emperor Titus Flavius Domitian. The emperor demanded to be worshiped as 'Lord and God,' and the refusal of the Christians to obey his creed led to severe persecution. According to historians, Domitian sent John to the Isle of Patmos.

Patmos is a small island that sits on the northernmost part of Greece's Dodecanese islands. John explained how it came about that he wrote the book of Revelation.

I, John, both your brother and companion in the tribulation and kingdom and patience of Jesus Christ, was on the island that is called Patmos for the word of God and for the testimony of Jesus

Christ. I was in the Spirit on the Lord's Day, and I heard behind me a loud voice, as of a trumpet, saying, "I am the Alpha and the Omega, the First and the Last," and, "What you see, write in a book and send it to the seven churches which are in Asia: to Ephesus, to Smyrna, to Pergamos, to Thyatira, to Sardis, to Philadelphia, and to Laodicea." Then I turned to see the voice that spoke with me. And having turned I saw seven golden lampstands, and in the midst of the seven lampstands One like the Son of Man, clothed with a garment down to the feet and girded about the chest with a golden band. His head and hair were white like wool, as white as snow, and His eyes like a flame of fire; His feet were like fine brass, as if refined in a furnace, and His voice as the sound of many waters; He had in His right hand seven stars, out of His mouth went a sharp two-edged sword, and His countenance was like the sun shining in its strength. And when I saw Him, I fell at His feet as dead. But He laid His right hand on me, saying to me, "Do not be afraid; I am the First and the Last. I am He who lives, and was dead, and behold, I am alive forevermore. Amen. And I have the keys of Hades and of Death. Write the things which you have seen, and the things which are, and the things which will take place after this. The mystery of the seven stars which you saw in My right hand, and the seven golden lampstands: The seven stars are the angels of the seven churches, and the seven lampstands which you saw are the seven churches." (Revelation 1:9–20)

Our guide told us that John had lived in a house near the seashore, but prayed in a cave, where he met with God. It was also in the cave where God told John to write down what He revealed to him. The guide then said, 'this is the place where he met with Jesus one morning during his quiet time. Jesus showed him what will happen at the end of days and told him to write it down.' He was told twice to write it down; 'What you see, write in a book ...' (Revelation 1:11), and 'Write the things which you have seen, and the things which are, and the things which will take place after this' (Revelation 1:19).

Just imagine that.

John was at the right place—the place of prayer. He separated himself from people and responsibilities and found a place where he could be alone with God. It was during those moments that he saw and met with Jesus as He spoke to him. The same Jesus who spoke to John will speak to us too. Jesus told him to write down what he saw, heard and experienced in his quiet time. He wrote that down in his 'journal,' which is still read and studied today, almost 2,000 years later. Jesus also told him what would happen at the end of days. The Bible is God's story and revelation from Genesis through to Revelation. It was not written just to provide information and history about a distant people who served God. It was given to us, by God, so that it would help us find our way to Him through the light of His Word. When we read the Word, we are reading what God 'wrote' Himself through various prophets and instruments.

God wrote on the tablets of stone, the Law and commandments and gave it to Moses, so that he might teach that to the Israelites (Exodus 24:12).

God told Moses to write down the words that God had spoken to him on Mount Sinai (Exodus 34:27).

God told Habakkuk to write down the vision and make it plain on tablets (Habakkuk 2:2).

God told John to write down what he saw in a book and send it to the seven churches which are in Asia (Revelation 1:11, 19).

Likewise, it might be a good idea for us to write down all the things that God reveals to us and says to us in our quiet times.

Writing It Down

Some years ago, I began journaling but stopped after a while. As I was developing the *Connected* material, God spoke to me about journaling and I started to do it once again. When I go back and read what I wrote before, I can see how God worked in and through my life. I discovered that writing down and responding to Scripture in my journal made it more memorable. 'Blessed is the man who listens to me, watching daily at my gates, waiting at the posts of my doors' (Proverbs 8:34). There are many benefits in keeping a personal devotional journal. Keeping a journal is a constant reminder of how God has met your needs, and how He is at work in your life.

Where do I Start?

If you have never used a journal, you may wonder where to start. You need a pen and writing pad or notebook. You open the book and write down the first thoughts that come to mind as you read and meditate in your quiet time. You should just write freely about the things that you are thinking about, the things that are on your mind or the questions that you may have. It is just another avenue that you can use to process the thoughts in your mind and heart while at the same time taking notes of your journey and testimony for future reference.

What do I Write in my Journal?

Gordon MacDonald, in his book *Ordering Your Private World*, explains:

I write in my journal almost every day, but I am not overly disturbed if an occasional day passes without an entry. And what is in there? An account, of things that I accomplished in the preceding day, people I met, things I learned, feelings I experienced, and impressions I believe God wanted me to have. I include prayers, insights that come from the reading the Bible and other spiritual literature, and concerns I have about my own personal behavior. All of this is part of listening to God. As I write, I am aware that what I am writing may actually be what God wants to tell me.[50]

What to do when God reveals a new spiritual truth to your heart, or an understanding of Himself? I suggest that you do the following:

- Write down the key Scripture verse or passage in your journal. Writing it down helps to impress the verse on your mind and helps you to recall them later in the day. You can also write them down as they appear in various translations.
- Take the time to meditate and reflect on the truth of the verse. You might want to ask yourself some questions, as indicated in the list below.
- Write down a prayer—to ask the Lord to help you apply the truths that you have learned.
- Watch to see how God uses the truth in your life.

Questions to Reflect on:

- Who is the author of the passage?
- Who are the recipients of the Word or teaching?
- What is happening in the passage?
- What does the author intend to communicate?
- When do these events take place?

- Where do these events take place?
- Why do these events take place?
- How do these events occur?
- How are these events relevant to my life?

Questions for Personalizing:

- Is there a warning or a sin that I need to be aware of?
- Is there an example to follow?
- Is there a command to obey?
- Is there an invitation to respond to?
- What is God asking me to do right now?
- What person or concern has God given to me to pray for?
- What struggles do I have at the moment?
- What is this passage teaching me about God, Father, Son and Holy Spirit?
- What is it teaching me about the ways and purposes of God?
- What liberty will I experience if I respond to this verse?
- How will this affect or impact my life, marriage or workplace if I respond to it?
- Identify the adjustments that you will have to make.

The Bible is not a book that we have to read; it is a book that we have to live. God has something to say to you through His Word, a truth that—when practised faithfully— will make a difference in your life. Failing to be obedient to God's Word is a lot like a person who looks in a mirror, sees an imperfection in their clothing or a smear on their face, and walks away without correcting it.

In Closing

We have come to the end of the most intimate part of our devotional time. You have read the Bible, listened and responded to God through personal prayer and written down the insights, values, principles and truths that you have received from Him. In short, you have taken the time to read the Scriptures, reflect on some observations, made the decision to personalize and apply the truths and insights that you have gained and are ready to pray about it and bring your own needs before Him in prayer.

STEP FIVE

PERSONAL PRAYER

May God be gracious to us and bless us and make his face shine upon us.

Psalm 67:1 (*English Standard Version*)

Prayer makes a godly man, and puts within him the mind of Christ, the mind of humility, of self-surrender, of service, of pity, and of prayer. If we really pray, we will become more like God, or else we will quit praying.

E.M. Bounds[51]

I love traveling to Israel. One of my favourite places along the Mediterranean Sea is Jaffa, known as Joppa in biblical days. It was from Jaffa's harbour that Jonah ran away from God's call for his life. Instead of sailing to Nineveh and taking the message of repentance to the people, he boarded a ship headed to Tarshish.

Running away from God's call was the easy option. I am sure that three days in the belly of a fish got his attention (Jonah 1:3). It was from Lydda that Peter *ran into* Jaffa when God used him to restore Dorcas's life to her (Acts 9:36–42). As a result the news of the miracle the Lord had done spread through Jaffa, and many believed in the Lord (v. 42). It was in Jaffa, at the house of Simon the Tanner, where Peter received the vision to go to the house of Cornelius in Caesarea, 30 miles north on the Mediterranean Sea (Acts 10). As a result Peter traveled to Cornelius and saw how God would begin to extend the kingdom even to the gentiles. Once again, as a result of Cornelius' conversion, many responded positively to the message of salvation in Jesus.

The disciples were a praying people. They watched how Jesus prayed, and asked Him to teach them to pray also (Luke 11:1). They often met to pray together and waited upon God in prayer, even as they anticipated the coming of the Holy Spirit (Acts 1). It was in Jaffa that Peter went up to the rooftop in the middle of the day to observe a time of prayer (Acts 10:9). He was not seeking God's guidance or something specific when he went up those stairs to pray. He was simply going into the presence of God at his normal, set time for prayer. He enjoyed fellowship and communion with God at a set time, his quiet time.

It is clear from this passage that we must allow God to remove our prejudices (preparing our heart to receive) and if we really want to hear from God or receive His guidance, we must put ourselves in the place where He can communicate with us. It was during his time of prayer and communion with God that the Spirit revealed the next step Peter should take. If we are in constant communion with God, we will become more sensitive to His promptings. We will be able to discern between our own desires and His will and respond to Him accordingly.

The example of Peter teaches us that God's ways are not our ways. God wants to be part of our lives even when we are running away from the Holy Spirit. He wants to entrust to us the bigger picture, which only He can see. He wants to bless our life in all circumstances. He also desires to share His blessing with others around us through the unfolding of His plan and purpose. So, in prayer the first thing we should do is to find God's plan and purpose; the second thing is to make that purpose our prayer. We want to find out what God is thinking, and respond to it, and claim that it shall be done on earth as it is in heaven (Matthew 6:10). It is clear that three key elements set the agenda and guide our time of prayer:

- Being *with* Him
- Receiving *from* Him
- Working *for* Him

Being with Him

First, we are called to 'be with Him,' in His Presence and to commune with Him. It is when we set aside time for prayer, unhurried time daily, our minds fresh, and our spirit sensitive. It is when we get to be alone that we find out we are not alone, because God is already waiting for us. I have explained these thoughts in more detail in my book *Running on Empty*.[52]

Receiving from Him

Second, we are called to 'receive from Him.' Our quiet times are the place where we can train our ears to hear from God. Prayer is how we talk to God while reading the Word and listening to the Holy Spirit is how we receive from God. We need an ear to hear, a tongue to pray, and an eye to look out for God's work around us.

Nicolas Herman was a monk who worked in the kitchen of a monastery in Paris. He became known as Brother Lawrence, who inspired a little book entitled *The Practice of the Presence of God*. Joyce Huggett, in her book *Finding God in the Fast Lane*, wrote about one incident in his life.

He related that he encountered God while cobbling the monks' shoes and while on business trips. One of his responsibilities was to buy the monastery's supply of wine, which involved traveling by boat from Paris to Burgundy and Auvergne and bringing back with him the barrels of wine. He disliked these trips partly because of his disability, which restricted his mobility. He could move about the boat only by rolling himself over the wine casks.

Even so we find him rejoicing in God's intervention in these potentially irksome transactions. He simply asked God to partner with him, trusted that He would do so, and watched to see how all the details would be woven into a beautiful pattern. Like Paul, he seemed to be able to say with integrity, 'I am ready for anything anywhere ... there is nothing that I cannot master with the One who gives me strength' (Philippians 4:13).[53] What do we receive? We receive His written Word (Exodus 24:12), insights, new spiritual truths, perspective, guidance and strength for our next task.

Working for Him

Third, we are called to 'work with Him' in prayer. Let me give you a few insights I have learned over the years which I have found helpful in my prayer time.

Insight 1—My personal time of prayer includes my 'response prayer,' as explained in previous steps. My focus is on myself, with the intention to worship Jesus, thank Him for all His goodness, confess any known sin and pray for all my own personal needs on my prayer list. I work to clear out all the harmless issues that clutter and corrupt. I sanctify myself to become a better follower of Jesus (John 17:19). I also pray about the four things that Jesus prayed for Himself (John 17:1–8) and allow the Holy Spirit to guide and direct my prayer. I want *to glorify* Him in all I do. I want *to finish* the work He has given me to do. I want *to manifest* His name. I want *to deliver* His Word.

It is during this time that real and genuine change, true transformation takes place that would be visible for all to see and experience when they come into contact with us.

Insight 2—During this time my focus moves away from myself to the people whom God has uniquely brought into my life, and the ministry that God has given me. I pray for the people who are in my life, and my circles of concern. I also pray for wisdom, direction and help for the various aspects of my ministry.

Insight 3—The focus shifts to the Great Commission and the world, the burden-bearing work of God and His people, through prayer, to live and act like Jesus, and to witness to others.

Helen Ewan

Helen Ewan, a Scottish girl from Glasgow, died in 1932 at the age of 22. She was an ordinary person, yet she left behind an extraordinary legacy. Her life and daily routine were filled with the glory and presence of God. She spread the fragrance of the Lord Jesus wherever she went and had a marked influence on the people she encountered. As a young adult, she spent hours each day reading the Bible and praying. She believed the words of Robert Murray M'Cheyne, who once said, '*It is the look that saves, but it is the gaze that sanctifies.*'[54] Helen gazed with rapture into the face of her Lord. Her life had made such an impact on others that hundreds attended her funeral.

Helen knew how to seek after God because it was modeled to her by her parents. Her entire family's existence revolved around the life of the Lord Jesus. James Stewart, a family friend and the biographer who wrote her story, was undoubtedly touched and challenged by her life and example. In his book about her life, *She Was Only 22*, he recalls that he always saw three worn Bibles on the table in the living room when he visited the Ewan family. Helen Ewan's parents were poor, but left a rich legacy, as Stewart related:

Although she died at the age of 22, all of Scotland wept. I know hundreds of missionaries all over the world who wept and mourned for her. She had mastered the Russian language and was expecting to labour for God in Europe. She had no outstanding personality; she never wrote a book, nor composed a hymn; she was not a preacher and never traveled more than 200 miles from her home. But when she died, people wrote about her life story. Although she died so early in life, she had led a great multitude to Jesus Christ.

She arose early each morning at about 5 o'clock to study God's word, to commune, and to pray. She prayed for hundreds of missionaries. Her mother showed me her diary—one of her diaries—and there were at least 300 different missionaries for whom she was praying. It showed how God had burdened that young heart with a ministry of prayer. She had the date when she started to pray for a request and then the date when God answered her petition. She had a dynamic prayer life that moved God and moved man. I was talking one day with two university professors in London City. We were talking about dynamic Christianity, when one of them suddenly said, "Brother Stewart, I want to tell you a story." And then he told me that in Glasgow University there was a remarkable young lady, who, wherever she went on that campus, she left the fragrance of Christ behind her. For example, if the students were telling dirty stories, someone would say, "Sh-hh, Helen is coming—quiet." And then she passed by and unconsciously left the power behind her. The University professor told me how in their prayer meetings, they could always tell when this young lady entered the room. She did not even have to take part in prayer. The moment she entered the room, the whole of the meeting was revolutionized by the mighty power of God. "And" said that professor, "she led many of those students to Jesus Christ." She was the most significant power for God that he ever knew in his life. I said, "Sir, that could only be one person. That was Helen Ewan." He said that was the name of the young lady. I have been out on the streets of Glasgow at midnight, in the awful cold winter night giving out tracts and doing personal soul winning, and as I have been going home, I have seen Helen Ewan with her arms around a poor drunken harlot, and telling her of Jesus and His love. Friends, she led a great multitude to Jesus Christ.

And when I went years later to the place of her burial, one of the gravediggers said, "Preacher, I'll never forget when that young lady was buried here. When I was burying that body, I felt the presence of God all over this place." One night we were all having a social evening together, young people rejoicing in the Lord, and having a good time, when my wife said, "Is that Helen Ewan's photograph on the mantlepiece?" Suddenly there was dead silence, and she said, "Jim, have I said anything wrong?" The laughter ceased and one by one, without a word, we dropped down on our knees and began to pray! Think of it, years after she had gone home to heaven, her name was so magical and so powerful. Oh, friends, I believe that this spiritual life is for every child of God![55]

What was the Secret of her Life?

The question that comes to mind: what was the secret of her life? How could a young lady that never preached a sermon or sung a solo, never traveled more than two hundred miles away from her home; impacts people from all over the world? In my reading and research I have come across a Blog that was posted on *Girl's Radiant Walk* that perfectly summarizes the life of Helen Ewan and the secret of her short but powerful life. [56]

First, her whole being *radiated* the glory of God.

Second, she had a deep *appetite* for the Word of God and penetrated deep into spiritual truths. As she studied the Word of God, under the illuminating guidance of the Holy Spirit, He revealed hidden treasures of the Lord to her (John 16:14–15). This made her heart dance with joy. Helen would regularly stop Christians in the street and, with a radiant face, tell them of some Scripture in which she had found a new picture of her blessed Redeemer. These friends often left her presence weeping. They said, 'We have seen Jesus; we have looked into His glorious face.' The awe of God remained upon their souls throughout the remainder of the day. She knew the Lord in such a deeply intimate way.

Third, she is an *example* to all Christians. She rose each morning at around 05:00 a.m. to commune with her Lord. She would not put on the heat in her cold little room or seek to make herself comfortable in any way. She felt that she would be more alert in the cold. And, besides, those for whom she prayed in foreign lands were not living in comfort. She would pray for herself, her family and, without fail, sinners around her and in distant lands. She was an intercessor who presented missionaries and ministers before the throne of grace as they labored in the field of souls. No wonder the lamentation on her death. At far-off mission stations, British missionaries grieved on hearing the news. Alas, who would bear them up so faithfully at the throne of grace now? Who would step into this gap and take her place?

Fourth, she *consulted* the Lord on all things. All through the day she sought God's guidance in matters small and great. It was no small thing for her to shop for some personal item and she might seem to pause in front of the store to seek His guidance before going in for a length of ribbon. She was compelled to please Him in all things and she would not be led by the traditions of people. That no doubt explains the remark of her friends that Helen was always dressed right.

Fifth, she had *compassion* for the lost. Helen's seeking after lost souls also puts us all to shame. In this way, more than one soul who was burdened with the cares of this life and bowed down with the weight of sin and despair was led to know the Savior as Helen pointed her to the Lamb of God under a lamppost or while waiting at the streetcar's stop.

Last, she *resembled* God. Helen carried the fragrance of Christ with her. She manifested the power of the Spirit. Her body was a walking temple of the Holy Spirit. Thus, wherever she went the power of God was manifested. When she entered any service, the atmosphere was charged with His power immediately.

What about you?

Can the same be said of your prayer life?

STEP SIX

PERSONALIZED OBEDIENCE

Therefore, whoever hears these sayings of Mine, and does them, I will liken him to a wise man who built his house on the rock: and the rain descended, the floods came, and the winds blew and beat on that house; and it did not fall, for it was founded on the rock.
Matthew 7:24–25

God is God. Because He is God, He is worthy of my trust and obedience. I shall only find rest in His holy will and what He can do is indescribably beyond my greatest thoughts.
Elisabeth Elliot[57]

A couple of years ago I was invited to speak at the morning and evening services of a local church in Pretoria. I got up early that morning to prepare myself for the services. The Bible reading in my devotional that morning was in the Gospel of John, chapter 14. My attention was especially drawn to verses 21 through 23:

He who has My commandments and keeps them, it is he who loves Me. And he who loves Me will be loved by My Father, and I will love him and manifest Myself to him. Judas (not Iscariot) said to Him, "Lord, how is it that You will manifest Yourself to us, and not to the world?" Jesus answered and said to him, "If anyone loves Me, he will keep My word; and My Father will love him, and We will come to him and make Our home with him."

Jesus said that if we love Him, treasure His word and obey it, then the Father and the Son will share Their love with us, manifest Themselves to us and make Their home with us. Our experience with God ought to go deeper and deeper, and it will as we yield in obedience to the Spirit of Truth and permit Him to teach us and guide us every day.

If we love God and obey Him, He will reveal and manifest Himself to us in a deeper way each day.

I incorporated my thoughts on the passage in the service that Sunday morning and I felt excited about the new insights I had gained regarding that passage. After the service I got into my car to drive back home when God spoke to me. He simply told me to go to the hospital and pray for someone. I thought for a moment about the family gathering for the send-off at our home for a couple who were flying out to Russia that evening and even of the time that I needed to prepare for the evening service, but I couldn't shake off the awareness that I needed to go to a hospital and pray for someone. The Holy Spirit gently reminded me of the words of Jesus in John 14 and the message I just preached; '*If anyone loves Me, he will keep My word*.'

So, I drove to the nearest hospital but the person whom the Lord had impressed upon my heart was not there. I found him sitting in a wheelchair at the second hospital that I visited, both his arms in plaster. He had been involved in a vehicle accident and could not use his hands and arms. He was so very concerned about his wife, who had visited him the previous day, as he did not know whether she had made it back home safely. They lived in an unsafe area and she had to take a taxi to and from the hospital. I was able to lend him the use of my phone and he could speak to her. We talked for a while and I prayed for him before I left. God used my obedience to bless another who was in need. But I also received a blessing that day; I received the joy of being able to help someone.

I also understood that my obedience laid the foundation for yet another encounter with Jesus as He promised in His Word to manifest Himself to those who obey Him.

Obedience

If we truly want to experience and encounter God in our lives, we must deal with the word 'obedience.' It is not the most popular word in our vocabulary. We live in a society that constantly challenges the norms and standards of any religious system. Obedience is much more than simply following some rules; it's a state of the mind and heart.

It is of the utmost importance to experiencing God. By missing this truth, we miss the power and blessing of complete obedience. The blessing of obedience is our connection with a loving, protective and caring heavenly Father Who desires more than anything to give us a rich and fulfilling life! He wants to love us, manifest Himself to us and make His home within us.

Looking Back

We have already seen that when we come to our quiet time, to meet with God, we need to prepare for the encounter. As we approach our time with Him, we must remember and reflect on what God has been saying to us lately. He does not speak in isolation. His prompting is not detached from what He is already doing in and around us. He knows what He is doing and where He is going. The question that we must answer is, 'What has God said to me recently?' and 'Have I responded to Him through obedience and have

I adjusted my life to His will?' We must deal with these questions before we enter into the presence of God, in order to truly encounter Him.

Looking Up

Having a willing and obedient heart is critical when it comes to hearing God speak through His Word. You must answer God before you begin your journey of reading His Word and listening to His Voice. You may say, 'How can I give an answer before I know what He said?' or, 'If I don't know what God is saying, how can I respond?' Listen carefully: you must be able to give your answer *before* you even hear God speak. If you have made the decision to make Jesus Christ your Savior and Lord, then you should only have one answer, 'YES, Lord.' Before you even hear Him speak, you must be ready to answer 'yes.' The Lord will speak freely to those who have a heart willing to obey Him. So, what is your answer? If there is any hesitation in your heart, do not expect God to speak to you. Have you accepted the fact that God is Lord? If the answer is no, then He cannot trust you with an assignment. He cannot entrust to you the greater things of the kingdom.

So, take a moment to recognize God's right to your life and let Him know that your answer is 'yes,' no matter what He says. You will be astonished to see what freedom that brings to your personal walk with the Lord and your understanding of His Word. When God knows you are ready to respond to His task, He will talk to you about what is on His heart.

Looking Forward

The most important part of our quiet time is personalized obedience or the practical application of the truths that we have learned. In our time with God we read the Scriptures, listen to His voice, respond in prayer and write down the thoughts and insights that we have gained. However, we can still decide not to respond in obedience to God's Word. That is why it is so important to settle the issue of whether you are ready to respond affirmatively to what God is about to say or reveal to you, before you even start with your quiet time. If you are ready to respond to God's Word, it is time to personalize or apply what you have learned from your devotional time.

I have found it helpful to reflect on the following questions to process and apply the truths that I have learned:

- What did God say to me today?
- What is the specific application to my life?
- Am I going to do it?
- Who is going to hold me accountable?

In Closing

Jesus turned to those who were following Him and said, 'Why do you call Me "Lord, Lord," and do not do the things that I say?' (Luke 6:46). You see, calling Christ 'Lord' does not mean He *is the* Lord of your life. We can fool ourselves into thinking that Christ will give us all things because we are Christians. That is just not true. Our obedience to God's will reveals the true standing of our relationship with God. If you obey God's Word, you enjoy greater encounters and fellowship with Him. However, if you do not obey God's Word, He will become quiet. If you have not done the last thing Christ said, why would He tell you something new?

What you *do* concerning the things of the Word reveals what you *believe* about God, no matter what you say. If you have not obeyed the last thing He said, He most likely will not say anything else until you understand His lordship.

So, go back and see if there are unresolved issues in your life—things that have been left undone. Ask the Lord to help you put into practise what He has already been saying to you in His Word.

I want to close with the same passage that we started with about what God told Moses: the four requirements Moses and the others had to comply with to meet with Him (Exodus 19:1–14). First, they had *to be willing to obey* (Exodus 19:3–8). Second, they had *to be sensitive to listen* (Exodus 19:9). Third, they had *to sanctify and consecrate* their hearts (Exodus 19:10–14). Last, they had *to show deep respect* for God's presence (Exodus 19:21–23). And as a result of their obedience, God came down to meet with them (Exodus 19:16–19).

It was when Moses entered into His presence that God came down to meet with Him (Exodus 24; 34). Moses was blessed in many ways. He heard the voice of God. He met God face to face. He received God's commission for his next task. He was changed and transformed in God's presence.

Jesus once entered Bethany, a small village near Jerusalem, and stayed in the home of Martha and Mary. Mary rushed to sit at the feet of Jesus while Martha was preparing the meal in the kitchen. At some point Martha complained to Jesus about Mary, who was not helping her to serve the guests. Jesus answered and said to her; 'Martha, Martha, you are worried and troubled about many things. But one thing is needed, and Mary has chosen that good part that will not be taken away from her' (Luke 10:41–42). Mary made Jesus her first priority and Jesus said that she would receive a blessing that would not be taken away from her.

Likewise, when we make Jesus our first priority, He will make Himself known to us, and give us spiritual blessings that no one can take away from us. A word from Jesus is life-changing and transforming. If we fast-forward to John

12:1–8, when Jesus entered Bethany again a few years later, we see how Mary and Martha had changed. First, we see that they both made supper, and Martha served (without complaining this time, v. 2). Second, we see that Mary's devotion was even more intense when she took a pound of very costly oil of spikenard to anoint the feet of Jesus and wiped His feet with her hair (v. 3).

Isn't that the ultimate goal of our quiet time? To meet and have an encounter with God. To receive from Him a blessing that will not be taken away from us. We receive His insights, His words; secure His presence as we go throughout the day and in doing so we are transformed; we are changed. God loves us, and wants to bless, and tabernacle with us. However, our response to Him today determines our encounter with Him tomorrow.

It is my prayer that these simple steps and guidelines from *Connecting Time* will help you to get into the habit of making time for God and experiencing Him more intimately than you ever thought possible.

It's time to get ready for a brand-new experience with God.
It's *Connecting Time!*

NOTES

1. S.D. Gordon, *Trysting Time* (London, U.K.: Oliphants), 7

2. Howard and Geraldine Taylor, *The Spiritual Secret of Hudson Taylor* (New Kensington, Penn.: Whitaker House, 1997), n.p.

3. Edwin and Lillian Harvey, *They Knew their God* (Hampton, Tenn.: Harvey Christian Publishers, 1974; 2003), n.p.

4. Arthur T. Pierson, *George Müller of Bristol* (London, U.K.: Pickering and Inglis Ltd.; and G. Fred Bergin, *Autobiography of George Müller: a Million and a Half in Answer to Prayer* (Denton, Tx.: Westminster Literature Resources Inc., 2003), n.p.

5. Roger Steer's *A Living Reality* contains George Müller's Experience of God (London: Hodder and Stoughton, 1985), 61–62

6. Jim Downing, *Meditation* (Colorado Springs, Colo.: Dawson Media, 2001), 8–9

7. Bobby Moore, *Your Personal Devotional Life* (Southaven, Miss.: The Kings Press, 2001), 2

8. Kathleen White, *C.T. Studd, Cricketer and Crusader* (Basingstoke, U.K.: Marshall Pickering, 1985), Back page

9. Available at https://en.wikipedia.org/wiki/Charles_Studd

10. Available at https://thenextweb.com contributors/2019/01/30/digital-trends-2019-every-single-stat-you-need-to-know-about-the-internet/

11. Available at https://www.networkworld.com/

article/3092446/we-touch-our-phones-2617-times-a-day-says-study.html

12. S.D. Gordon, *Trysting Time* (London, U.K.: Oliphants), 5

13. Ibid., 7

14. E.F. and L. Harvey, *Kneeling We Triumph*, Book Two (Pensacola, FL: Harvey Christian, 1971), 83

15. Bobby Moore, *Your Personal Devotional Life* (Southaven, Miss.: The King's Press, 2001), 8

16. Francois Carr, *Running on Empty* (Book in publication process with The Connected Life Ministries).

17. Peter V. Deison, *Time with God* (Grand Rapids, Mich.: Discovery Series, 1992), 15

18. John Ortberg, *Soulkeeping* (Grand Rapids, Mich.: Zondervan, 2014), 20

19. Bobby Moore, *Your Personal Devotional Life* (Southaven, Miss.: The King's Press, 2001), 69–74

20. Available at https://www.azquotes.com/quote/824006

21. E.F. and L. Harvey, *How They Prayed*, Volume Two (Richmond, KY.: Harvey Christian, 2014), 9–10

22. Ibid., 18–19

23. Francois Carr, *The Call* (Pretoria, South Africa: The Connected Life Ministries, 2021), 35–39

24. Francois Carr, *Running on Empty* (Book in publication process with The Connected Life Ministries).

25. Available at https://www.pinterest.com/pin/796574252820845341/

26. Charles F. Swindoll, *Moses* (Nashville, TN: Thomas Nelson, 1999), 267–269

27. Francois Carr, *The Call* (Pretoria, South Africa: The Connected Life Ministries, 2021), 46–52

28. Francois Carr, *Running on Empty* (Book in publication process with The Connected Life Ministries).

29. E.F. and L. Harvey, *How They Prayed*, Volume Two (Richmond: Harvey Christian, 2014), 7–8

30. Ibid., 18

31. Ibid., 78
32. Lois Tverberg, *Reading the Bible with Rabbi Jesus* (Grand Rapids, Mich.: Baker Books, 2017), 24–25
33. Ibid., 25
34. Lois Tverberg, *Listening to the Language of the Bible* (Holland, Mich.: Ein Gedi Resources, 2004), 87–88
35. Ibid., 88
36. Brother Lawrence, *Practice the Presence of God* (Pa.: Judson), n.p.
37. Charles Swindoll, *Intimacy with the Almighty* (Nashville, Tenn.: J. Countryman, 1999), 38
38. Ibid., 39
39. E.F. and L. Harvey, *Kneeling We Triumph*, Book Two (Hampton, Tenn.: Harvey Christian, 1971), 78
40. Francois Carr, *Spiritual Breathing* (Book in publication process with The Connected Life Ministries, 2021).
41. Bruce Bennie, *Andrew Murray: Theologian of the Heart* (Morphett Vale, South Australia, 2004), 19
42. Francois Carr, *The Call* (Pretoria, South Africa: The Connected Life Ministries, 2021), 83, 84, 95, 96
43. Oswald Chambers, *My Utmost For His Highest* (Uhrichsville, Ohio: Barbour, 1935), n.p.
44. L.B. Cowman, *Streams in the Desert* (Grand Rapids, Mich.: Zondervan, 1999), n.p.
45. Henry and Richard Blackaby, *Experiencing God Day by Day* (Jonesboro, Ga.: B & H), n.p.
46. *Our Daily Bread* available at Our Daily Bread.org.
47. Robert Murray M'Cheyne, Bible Reading Plan available at bibleplan. Org/plans/mcheyne/
48. Warren Wiersbe, *God Isn't In A Hurry* (Nottingham, England: Crossway Books, 1994), 39
49. Francois Carr, *Spiritual Breathing* (Book in publication process by The Connected Life Ministries, 2021).

50. Gordon MacDonald, *Ordering Your Private World* (Crowborough, East Sussex, U.K.: Highland Books, 1985), 171, 179, 181

51. Available at https://www.crosswalk.com/faith/ spiritual-life/inspiring-quotes/31-prayer-quotes-be-inspired-and-encouraged.html

52. Francois Carr, *Running on Empty* (Book in publication process with The Connected Life Ministries, 2021).

53. Brother Lawrence in Joyce Huggett, *Finding God in the Fast Lane* (Guildford, Surrey, U.K.: Eagle, 1993), 27

54. Francois Carr, *Connecting My Family with God* (Pretoria, South Africa: The Connected Life Ministries, 2021), 9–10. See also James Stewart, *She was only 22* (Asheville, NC:Revival Literature, 2004), 1–12

55. James Stewart, *She was only 22* (Asheville, NC.: Revival Literature, 1966), n.p.

56. Read full blog published by Girls Radiant Walk on 3 April 2019 at https://www.girlsradiantwalk.com/helen-ewan-7-lessons-from-her-brief-but-beautiful-life/

57. Available at https://www.goodreads.com/author/ quotes/6264.Elisabeth_Elliot

LIST OF RECOMMENDED RESOURCES

DAILY DEVOTIONALS

Experiencing God Day by Day	Henry & Richard Blackaby
My Utmost for His Highest	Oswald Chambers
Streams in the Desert	Mrs. Charles Cowman
A Threefold Cord	Helena Garratt
The Daily Challenge	Edwin & Lillian Harvey
Walk with God	F.B. Meyer
The Divine Secret	Andrew Murray
God's Best Kept Secret	Andrew Murray
Morning by Morning	Charles Spurgeon
Evening by Evening	Charles Spurgeon
The Christian's Secret of a Holy Life	Hannah Whitall Smith

SUGGESTED READING

Running on Empty	Francois Carr
The Call	Francois Carr
Spiritual Breathing	Francois Carr
Trysting Time	S.D. Gordon
How they Prayed, Vols. 1 & 2	E.F. and L. Harvey
The Practice of the Presence of God	Brother Lawrence
Hearing God	Peter Lord
Ordering Your Private World	Gordon McDonald
Prevailing Prayer	D.L. Moody
Your Personal Devotional Life	Bobby Moore
Prayer Life and the Inner Room	Andrew Murray
Prayer, A conversation with God	Rosalind Rinker
She was only 22	James A. Stewart
The Prayer Factor	Sammy Tippit
Time Well Spent	Colin Webster

WHO IS FRANCOIS?

Francois Carr
Executive Director of Heart Cry in
South Africa and Founder of The
Connected Life Ministries

Francois Carr, BTH, MCC, D. Min, NDPB, is the Executive Director of Heart Cry in South Africa. He studied Personnel Management in Cape Town and followed a career as Personnel Officer in the South African Defense Force. During this time, he became involved in a youth ministry that prayed for revival in South Africa. He felt the call of the Lord into a revival-related ministry in November 1992 during a youth conference. He became the National Coordinator of Revival South Africa, which promoted the message of revival, while serving in a fulltime capacity as an officer in the Defense Force. He studied part-time and obtained the following degrees: Bachelor of Theology, Master's of Christian Counselling, and Doctor of Ministry.

As the National Coordinator of Revival South Africa, he planned and organized revival conferences throughout South Africa while still in full-time occupation until he felt led by the Lord to resign from his position (by then Lt. Col.) in the Defense Force to enter into full-time ministry. He stepped out in faith and became the Executive Director of Revival SA in June 1999. He founded a new ministry, Heart Cry SA, that focuses on helping people experience greater intimacy in their relationship with God and mentoring spiritual leaders at churches to become catalysts for revival. Heart Cry co-sponsors conferences in the USA, Europe, and Africa.

Francois is also the founder of The Connected Life Ministries, based in Boiling Springs, SC, and Connected—The Jesus Way, a disciple-based program that helps spiritual leaders to become disciple makers through duplication and multiplication. The Connected Life is focused on glorifying God and knowing Him in a personal and intimate way. The material is dedicated to mentoring and helping people on the journey to experiencing personal and spiritual awakening.

He is well known for his burden for revival and intimacy with God, and is a popular speaker in Africa, North America, the United Kingdom, Australia, and New Zealand. He has authored several books and articles on prayer, holiness, and revival.

He is married to Dorothea and has one daughter, Leoné, who is married to Werner Mostert. Francois currently resides in Pretoria, South Africa.

Books by Francois

Afrikaans:	English:
Gebed vir Herlewing	Prayer for Revival
Herlewing! Die Heerlikheid van God	Revival! The Glory of God
Is Jy Vol?	Running on Empty
My Tyd met Hom	Connecting Time
Die Rusgewer	The Rest-giver
Leef in kontak	The Call
Huisgodsdiens	Connecting my Family with God
	Spiritual Breathing

Contact Francois

- Retreats: Connected—The Jesus Way
- Revival Services: Personal Revival, Revival in the Family and Church
- Schools of Prayer: Connecting Time, Running on Empty, Family Devotions, The Voice of God, The Will of God, the Prayer of Power and the Power of Prayer, Prayer of Faith, How to live in His Presence, How do I change my community through my life of prayer?, Obstacles in my prayer life, Prayer and Revival.

Address: PO Box 90262, Garsfontein, Pretoria 0042
Email: fcarr@heartcrysa.co.za
Websites: South Africa—www.heartcrysa.com
          USA—www.connectedlifeministries.com

Be and become the follower you are meant to be

THE CALL

Francois Carr

Connecting my Life
with God's Call

**It is 30–33 A.D.,
Jesus is calling your
name.** *Follow Me, and
I will make you fishers
of men. Go therefore
and make disciples of
all nations.*

What would it be like to sit at the feet of Jesus: listening,
watching and learning more about His life, relationships,
ministry and kingdom? What will happen if we follow Him
wherever He leads and commissions us to go?

**In *The Call* we take a closer look at what it means to be with
Jesus, and follow Him, as we explore topics such as**

- To Be with Him
- To Hear Him Speak
- To Understand His Intentions
- To Receive His Empowerment

- To Respond with Trust
  and Obedience
- To Accomplish His Purposes
- To Rest and be Refreshed

God still calls us to Himself today, to follow Him to higher places
of devotion and worship, obedience, surrender, and mission.

Now available online at
www.heartcrysa.com or www.connectedlifeministries.com

90

GOD'S FORGOTTEN COMMAND

Francois Carr pleads for a return to family worship. Illustrated by means of examples of many great men and women in church history, this book answers these questions and demonstrates the influence for good that the practise of family worship has had throughout centuries. In addition the appendices contain examples of family worship sessions in action.

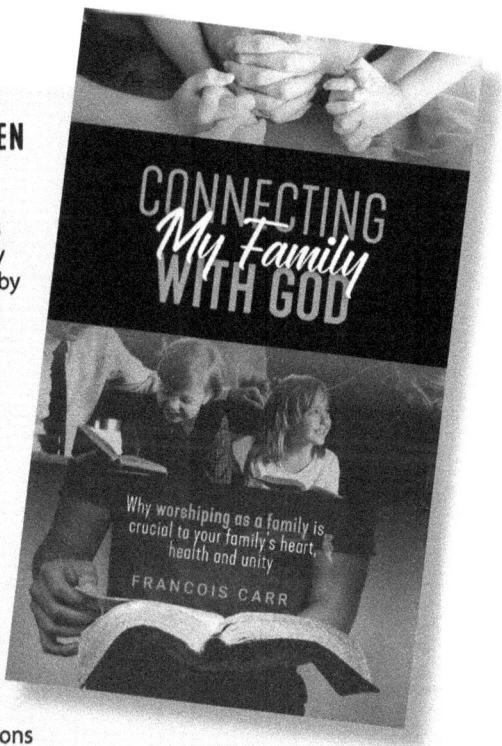

For many years we as parents have left the spiritual education of our children in the hands of schools and the church. With membership dwindling, some churches have discontinued their child and youth programs. God gave parents the responsibility of *connecting our families* with God.

Connecting my Family with God helps you to rediscover the joy of worshiping together as a family. Dr. Francois Carr shares personal lessons and discusses these topics:

- Why is Family Worship necessary?
- Why don't families worship together anymore?
- Common excuses for not having family worship?
- How do I prepare myself and my family?
- How do we worship as a family?
- What are the basic foundations of family worship?

Now available online at
www.heartcrysa.com or www.connectedlifeministries.com